No Ordinary Child

Unlocking the Leader Within Your Child

No Ordinary Child

Unlocking the Leader Within Your Child

by Denise Mira

WINEPRESS WP PUBLISHING

Impact Media
4819 Hunt St. NW
Gig Harbor WA 98335
www.denisemira.com
contact@denisemira.com

Cover illustration and book design by David McClure, Praetus.

Edited by Amy Ruff and Gwen Ellis.

The first printing of this book was in 2006 under the title *No Ordinary Child: Unlocking the Leader Within Your Child*.

The baby on the cover is wearing an FDA approved temporary dye tattoo. You can obtain these for fun at www.denisemira.com.

WinePress Publishing (PO Box 428, Enumclaw, WA 98022) functions only as book publisher. As such, the ultimate design, content, editorial accuracy, and views expressed or implied in this work are those of the author.

Unless otherwise noted, all Scriptures are taken from the Holy Bible, New International Version, Copyright © 1973, 1978, 1984 by the International Bible Society. Used by permission of Zondervan Publishing House. The "NIV" and "New International Version" trademarks are registered in the United States Patent and Trademark Office by International Bible Society.

Scripture references marked KJV are taken from the King James Version of the Bible.

Scripture references marked NKJV are taken from the New King James Version, © 1979, 1980, 1982 by Thomas Nelson, Inc., Publishers. Used by permission.

Scripture references marked TLB are taken from The Living Bible, © 1971 owned by assignment by Illinois Regional Bank N.A. (as trustee). Used by permission of Tyndale House Publishers, Inc., Wheaton, Illinois 60189. All rights reserved.

Scripture references marked RSV are taken from the Revised Standard Version of the Bible. © 1946, 1952, 1971 by the Division of Christian Education of the National Council of the Churches of Christ in the U.S.A. Used by permission.

ISBN 1-57921-855-5
Library of Congress Catalog Card Number: 2005910349

Printed in Colombia.

By faith Moses' parents hid him for three months after he was born, because they saw he was *no ordinary child*, and they were not afraid of the king's edict.

—Hebrews 11:23

DEDICATIONS

For the King and the kingdom! *Let this be written for a future generation, that a people not yet created may praise the LORD* (Psalms 102:18).

To Gregory—the love of my life, my greatest fan and fiercest comrade, outstanding leader, dedicated father, and world-changer. It is a privilege to march with you into all of our tomorrows.

To my boys and my new daughter Melissa—*I have no greater joy than to hear that my children are walking in the truth* (3 John 1:4). Your lives bring Daddy and me honor. Thank you.

To Cindy-Lee Marsh who walks on water regularly! Thank you so much for every little thing done with so much love. We will never be the same because of your sacrifice.

To Mom and Dad—Ralph and Donna Belitz—Thank you for the honorable example you lived out before me during my growing up years. I love you.

ACKNOWLEDGMENTS

To each of you precious saints of God here at Impact Church International and across the globe, who prayed me through this mammoth project—thank you!

Thank you, Carolyn and Jerry Tobias and Gwen and Daniel Brymer, for the impact you had on me as a young mother. You crashed into my perceptions and showed me a more excellent way.

Thank you, Sam and Jeanne Mayo and Dudley and Ann Daniel, for living kingdom on earth by blazing trails and laying tracks for me, my husband, our children, and those we love and walk with, and all those yet to come!

David and Veronica McClure—Marvelous comrades who helped bring this baby to birth! David, you have washed our feet with your amazing creative design and tireless labors of love on this project. Veronica, your encouragement was like wind in my sails!

Amy Ruff and Gwen Ellis—two of the sharpest tools in God's toolbox! I'm privileged to have had your hands on my project.

Elaine Wright Colvin—Two hours and a few e-mails made all the difference! Thank you for generously sharing your expertise, your heart, and your time with me.

CONTENTS

PREFACE

If I know anything at all, I know this: I am an imperfect woman with imperfect children living in a broken world, *but* I serve a sovereign God who has given me gargantuan vision for the future and destiny of my kids and *your* kids. I don't claim to be an expert, but my confidence rests in a God of the impossible who makes my dreams, from His Word, possible. I'm watching it happen in our lives, our home, and our children, and if there's any piece of the puzzle I can share to aid you in your quest to become all you can be as a *parent of leaders*, then my mission is accomplished!

Raise the Bar!

You are thinking too small when you consider the destiny of your child. It's human nature for us to mentally disqualify ourselves and our kids from the huge call God has on each of our lives.

Perhaps your hopes have been dashed in the past. When we get disappointed, what do we do? We dial down and lower our level of expectation. But we must refuse to live there! We must all rise above the level of past disappointments. It's time to turn up our thermostats. We are called to change the world.

"But we are without renown," some say, and "such a vision seems presumptuous and out of reach," say others. But I say, *"Let us dare to believe God!"*

Something in your spirit is throbbing. Somehow you sense there is more for your children. Something is telling you the standards in your home aren't enough. Something is telling you the standards in our churches aren't enough. For our children's sakes, let's raise the bar in our homes and in our churches.

It is an atrocity to leave a child to himself, wallowing in mediocrity while excellence is only a few steps away. What a pity! What a waste of potential! What lives remain unmoved by this beige approach to living! We must dare to believe God to keep His Word as we follow His pattern for raising our children. We can bank on these promises. Will you join me afresh in believing?

Our children are called to be agents of change. Our children are called to have an impact in the world. My prayer is that this book will impart to you an undying hope to believe for more with regard to your children than you ever have before. May you have hope that is tangible and real—hope that will bring change. May the words on these pages be like a missile: power-packed with a substance that, upon release, deposits an actual ingredient to transform the way you see yourself, your kids, and your God.

Where is the one who brings courage and breakthrough to create the valiant, fighting world-changers? Let it be us! We must dare to raise the bar and believe!

CHAPTER ONE

Where Is Moses When You Need Him?

God is preparing His heroes; and when the opportunity comes, He can fit them into their places in a moment, and the world will wonder where they came from.

—A. B. Simpson

Our world stands at an Exodus moment in history, and it is demanding a Moses generation to come forth and bring deliverance to a society held captive by sin. A huge and cavernous vacuum is begging to be filled. This hungry void, created by sin and by multitudes of New Testament believers who have blended in with the world, will not be left wanting forever. God is faithful and He will answer.

God's enduring plan to solve this dilemma is to use His body, the church, according to Ephesians 3:10–11: *His intent was that now, through the church* [that's us!], *the manifold wisdom of God should be made known to the rulers and authorities in the heavenly realms, according to his eternal purpose which he accomplished in Christ Jesus our Lord.* The problem is that numerous churches aren't making a difference or having an impact. In many cases, if such churches "went away," they wouldn't be missed by anyone without vested interests.

These believers must face the fact that they are not getting the job done. In many cases, their substance has been diluted and their edge has been blunted to such an extent that they are doing more harm than good in our present world. My burden is to see these believers awakened to their true condition and the condition of their families, thus rousing them to change. Consequently, may they dare to believe our awesome God to transform their lives to such a degree that they become the leaders for which our society is desperate. In turn, may they release their children to be the powerful weapons God intended them to be!

When Moses was born, the captive Hebrew people were trapped in a nightmare. Consider what Exodus 1:8–11 tells us: *A new king came to the throne of Egypt who felt no obligation to the descendants of Joseph. He told his people, "These [Israelites] are becoming dangerous to us because there are so many of them. Let's figure out a way to put an end to this . . ." So the Egyptians made slaves of the Israelites and put brutal taskmasters over them to wear them down under heavy burdens* (TLB). Ironically, the Israelites multiplied in the face of this mistreatment and oppression.

The alarmed Egyptians forced their Israelite slaves to endure greater toil. Eventually, Pharaoh instructed the Hebrew midwives to kill all Hebrew boys as soon as they were born, but to let the girls live. When this scheme was derailed by God-fearing midwives, Pharaoh became even more ruthless. He commanded all of his people to throw the newborn Hebrew boys into the Nile River.

Let's not skim over the words of the Bible, softening the text by excusing it away as from another time or another place and labeling it "irrelevant" to us today. To put this passage in clearer perspective, let's imagine for a moment that the city where you currently live is steadily altered by government intrusion. City officials are suddenly seeming to monitor your every move, tax every breath, and impose such stringent regulations that private industry becomes a thing of the past.

You find yourself evicted from the home you've poured your life savings into. Your husband is ordered to work in a local factory at half the minimum wage for twelve-hour shifts, seven days a week. The thought of another pregnancy strikes fear in your heart due to new regulations that all males must be killed at birth, and the sons you've already born seem to be walking on thin ice. Your once-happy dwelling place has become a house of bondage. This nightmare was the reality God's people in Egypt faced at this time.

> **The stage has been set, and the crisis created by sin's consequences demands a deliverer.**

Moses had to come! This rapid succession of critical events became a swirling vortex of groans from the earth, pulling violently upon Providence to provide a rescue and prevent the only alternative—destruction. Currently, we stand poised in the same place as Christians across the planet ponder their place in history's timeline. The stage has been set, and the crisis created by sin's consequences demands a deliverer. *Moses must come!* This time, however, it's not going to be just one man for one nation. It's going to be a crop of hundreds and thousands and millions of believers.

A Moses generation will emerge from within kingdom communities to impact the entire globe! It's not maybe; it's not if. It is happening even now. And you have been invited to participate. You have been summoned to raise, train, and prepare a kingdom of God carriers: vessels to bring freedom to captive people.

We must see our children not as pets or decor in our lives, nor simply as posterity or offspring to show off to the Joneses. We must have eyes to see our children and all those children around us as the deliverers God is calling them to be in this generation.

When you watch a busy playground or follow a school bus packed with vibrant youngsters, do you see what I see? Looking through the glass at the rows of newborns in the maternity ward, do you stand in awe? As you tiptoe in quietly to gaze at your sleeping child, does he or she just take your breath away? What do you see in your little one? I pray that God will let us see beyond the natural to the supernatural potential that He has deposited in our children!

These children are God's secret weapons. These are His plan for release of the prisoners. These are our prophets and apostles and evangelists and pastors and teachers in-the-making. These are our trustworthy bankers, honest lawyers, and decent businessmen of tomorrow. In the sea of little faces across the continents of the earth, sit mayors, governors, delegates, diplomats, and other individuals significant to the future of our societies.

Many, many children need to be told that they are extraordinary. Many, many moms and dads must look upon their children with new eyes, full of faith, because God creates *no ordinary child.* I don't care if they're Down Syndrome, labeled ADHD, or slow learning. I don't care if they're cross-eyed or if they walk with a limp. They may be foster kids, orphans, or truants. God makes only dynamic children with limitless potential, and it is up to us to unlock that potential and present leaders to God who will change our world.

> **You have been summoned to raise, train, and prepare a kingdom of God carriers: vessels to bring freedom to captive people.**

These are leaders who will go into every dark place and will impact our schools, our coffee shops, our banks, our neighborhoods, and every place human beings live and dwell in our burgeoning metropolises, suburban cities, and country towns. *This Moses generation will come forth!*

Just ordinary children won't be good enough to get the job done! So let it not be "good enough" for us parents to raise regular, tax-paying guys and gals with nice jobs and fine titles when they can become *so much more!* I would be deeply disappointed if my sons turned out to be dutiful, voting businessmen who can rock and roll in the marketplace, but who do nothing to change the world for Jesus Christ. We must aim higher! Let us resolve never to settle for normal in our homes. Let us resolve never to settle for normal in our children's ministries or our local churches. It's time to get on our knees until we are able to see the powerful promise that God has placed in our sons and daughters. We *must* be fully persuaded by this truth.

I hear many parents saying, "Oh, I wish my kids were godly!" But God does not answer wishes. He does not answer daydreams. Your bedtime prayers are not good enough to get your children where they need to go. I want to urge us to "pray" the price, "fast" the price, and do whatever it takes to get our kids where we say we want them to go!

We think nothing of giving our best for the professor, the boss, the company, and perfect strangers whom we service in our careers. Although unintentionally, it seems we often serve our children the leftovers of our human resources. Isn't it time we reorganize our priorities and employ out-of-the-ordinary methods in training up the ones entrusted to us by our Creator? Could it be that we will taste of the supernatural in a brand new way as we take a leap of faith in the direction of our children? I think so. I'm experiencing it firsthand in my home and reveling in the goodness of God.

My nine-year-old came to me recently with his twelve-year-old friend. They had a pressing matter they wanted to discuss. My son began, "Momma, I know there are things I have to work on in my life. We've talked about this, and I'm committed to this plan. Derek and I want to start a cell group." I tried not to reveal my surprise as I watched these two little men sincerely express the mature cry of their spirits. This interaction would perhaps have appeared abnormal to many parents, but I'm thinking, "This should be normal." What are we accepting as *normal* in our homes, with our children, that is *abnormal* when gauged by the Word of God? As a man, as a woman, as parents, as households, and as churches, what are we accepting as our standard of rule and practice as it relates to our kids?

> **What are we accepting as *normal* in our homes, with our children, that is *abnormal* when gauged by the Word of God?**

Ordinary men, women, and children will not win this world to Christ. Ordinary men, women, and children will not attract outsiders to the kingdom of God. Our children must turn heads for the right reasons. Philippians 2:14–16 applies perfectly to our kids (and to Mom and Dad!). *Do everything without complaining or arguing, so that you may become blameless and pure, children of God without fault in a crooked and depraved generation, in which you shine like stars in the universe as you hold out the Word of life.*

As this verse instructs, our families must not merely *do spiritual things*, but *apply this Word to our lives* as a means of impacting our corrupt generation; then we as men and women, along with our children, will shine in such a way as to attract the attention of the lost! Our children become living examples, flesh and blood representations of God's kingdom on earth! When our children are shining in glowing contrast to the herd going to hell, we can then hold out the Word of life to those observing and complimenting us on our incredible kids.

You may have already raised your children. You may be sitting there saying, "I blew it; my kid's forty." If our kids are at an age where it appears they have already been molded, or to say it another way, we didn't weed the garden of their lives, then we must summon fresh faith.

Lamentations 3:22–23 reminds us that *through the LORD'S mercies we are not consumed, because **His compassions fail not. They are new every morning**; great is [His] faithfulness* (NKJV). We cannot trust in the disheartening circumstances of our troubled children. We must allow God to stir our faith anew! We must ask Him to make us, as parents, the models that even our grown children need us to be, so they too can be transformed.

You may be without children. Still, for the sake of the church of Jesus Christ, as well as for our lost world, you need to understand and embrace this concept: all those noisy boys and girls flocking to their classrooms on Sunday are the world-changers that God is busy building! This vision fits into the New Testament pattern that we say we believe. We must have a corporate vision of biblical parenting and see our children as young leaders that we must train, because *where there is no vision, the people perish* (Proverbs 29:18, KJV). As a part of God's family, we've got to get this in our ethos. We don't have ordinary children running around our churches. We don't have ordinary children living in our households.

We must have eyes to see that our offspring are just like Moses, with huge calls to reach our lost world. Our role is crucial. We must do no less for our children than Moses' parents did for him, for we too are living in such desperate days.

We're living in Exodus times and a new king is ruling, and he does not know us (see Exodus 1:8). America is not alone in her struggle at this critical moment. Cultures across the globe are in a time when right is called wrong, wrong is called right, and tolerance is king. The atmosphere is ripe for God to discharge His weapons of rescue, the church of the living God: both us and our children.

I grieve as I see too many people disqualify children from their full inheritance *in this life* and in His kingdom to come. The nations of the earth are in crisis. The secure, mooring values of yesterday no longer seem to apply. Chaos reigns in lives, homes, churches, and governments. Millions seem to live on the edge of despair. It's time to rise up in our thinking and theology about childrearing. We must prepare an army of Moses-like leaders who will liberate those held captive by the darkness in our world today.

CHAPTER TWO

We Need a Revolution!

If you are not sure you are fighting for what is right, do not fight.
If you are sure, then no sacrifice is too great.
—Douglas MacArthur

I t's important for us to remember where we live and what's going on around us. We Christians in westernized cultures must not live in unreality. We must not teach our children to live in unreality, either. How I love this land called America, and I'm sure you feel the same about your homeland, but we can't be fooled by looking only at the surface of things. The stunning malls and dream communities, the array of fine restaurants, and the plethora of plush vehicles can hypnotize us from seeing the truth.

The truth is that America and much of this world is afflicted with many ills. America's cultural crisis is a warning to others. See how far a nation can stray from a God-fearing foundation! Consider the shame of abortion on demand, rampant manslaughter by drunk driving, increased domestic violence and child abuse, and the plagues of fatherless children and teen pregnancy. Ponder America's crisis of methamphetamine labs popping up everywhere, the sense of a looming volcanic eruption of credit card debt, the growing dilemma of identity theft, widespread gambling and pornography addiction, and the increase of alcohol and prescription drug use for emotional disorders. Contemplate the current heinous taxation by government agencies, increasing judicial tyranny in the courts, and an absence of character and integrity in public officials and industry heads.

The fact is, our nation is in serious trouble and our future hangs in the balance. To make matters worse, much of the church has become marginalized, is culturally irrelevant, and is not taken seriously by unbelievers. I believe George Whitefield's observation of England in the 1800s could be said about America today: "The church in England at this time is in a deep sleep and it will take a loud voice to wake them out of it!" I believe this voice will be a clarion call resounding from this Moses generation.

God intends our children to be the remedy for what's ailing our nation, yet many youth are living in a fantasy. It's my strong conviction that America's practice of dumbing down generations of young people keeps them as perpetual children in many ways. It seems our young men can barely write an essay, read a substantial book, or hold a job past their first few paychecks. Our sons' and daughters' lives are spent dressing well, eating well, and flipping through magazines and other mindless photo-laden nonsense. They feed on frivolous and meaningless Hollywood offerings, while forming their worldviews according to Aaron Spelling, Homer Simpson, or any number of celebrities featured on *Entertainment Tonight*. They are youngsters who don't know what's happening in the world beyond Hot Topic, Abercrombie and Fitch, or Starbucks. They live by feelings, experiences, and the latest offerings of Hotmail.com.

Is their penchant for pleasure any wonder when they've cut their teeth on television, videos, and happy church? Our young "disciples" are spiritual infants who sit for hours in classettes for Christianettes. In our day, it seems that if Bob Tomato isn't greeting them on Sunday mornings and the snack doesn't measure up, well, church was a drag. Let's be done putting sugar on everything to make it sweet to their taste, be it church meetings, household chores, hand-me-downs, homework, or breakfast. It's incumbent upon us as parents to make necessary adjustments in order to see our children become the leaders God intends for them to be. I'd say it's high time for a revolution.

We Need a Revolution at Home

It's up to us parents to create our own revolution in our homes for our sons and daughters. We don't have time to wait for someone else to do it. By then, it will be too late. A revolution is a complete and radical change. It implies the overthrow of governmental power, usually by forceful means. Then, a different system, made up of new leadership, is put in place. You've heard of the Russian, French, and Chinese Revolutions. The revolution I'm speaking of is much closer to home. Fasten your seat belt, because, guess what? You get to lead it!

> **It's up to us parents to create our own revolution in our homes for our sons and daughters. We don't have time to wait for someone else to do it. By then, it will be too late.**

In America's current culture, often it's the blind leading the blind. So few of today's parents were ever really trained to be moms and dads of kingdom kids. Many parents are ill-equipped and morally bankrupt in their parenting because their moms were busy working while pretending that "everything is gonna be okay" with the kiddies. Kids were left alone to raise themselves. Much of their "training" came from the television set. And *Leave it to Beaver* and *Father Knows Best* weren't the programs they were imbibing.

During the last several years we've watched the role of Anemic Dad played out in such television sitcoms as *Home Improvement* and *Everybody Loves Raymond,* not to mention the innumerable insipid characters stumping as the impotent heads of households, advertising everything from pain medication to laundry soap. These castrated men limp along to the drumbeat of their aggressive, decisive, and very capable wives. In each instance, Mom is running the show. These homes are dysfunctional and out of order—God's order. Not a good model for the next generation.

Conventional parenting just doesn't cut it for me. I'm sure I don't have to convince you, but just in case you need to be persuaded, simply eyeball most kids at the mall, bus stop, skate park, or city pool. There is rarely an adult to be found in their midst and mischief abounds. *Is this what you want for your children?* You're looking at the mainstream. The majority of the kids you see out and about represent what everybody's doing. Kinda scary, huh? It's scarier yet if your kids are currently blending in with that bunch.

Children were made to be parented: molded, shaped, and mentored. And to do that, parents must be present. Kids may *survive* being home alone, but they certainly won't thrive. God tells us in Deuteronomy 11:18–19 to *Fix these words of mine in your hearts and minds; tie them as symbols on your hands and **bind** them on your foreheads. **Teach** them to your children, **talking** about them when you sit at home and when you walk along the road, when you lie down and when you get up.* This demands a deliberate effort on our part! Verse 22 goes on to say, ***Carefully observe** all these commands I am giving you to follow,* and proceeds with some astounding promises of what we can expect if we'll follow the instructions. Revolution in our homes has a price tag. Are you willing to pay it?

Godly authority is a foreign principle to most children. It's time to teach our kids to understand the principle of their God-given covering, which protects them if taken seriously and if heeded: the voice of their father first, then mother, and then the elders of the local church. Teach them that when they choose to step out from under that covering, they are in serious danger. Encourage them to avoid multiple self-inflicted wounds by fully and faithfully embracing the boundaries and authorities which God has built into their lives.

The much-traveled road of the current American culture is sure to make a train wreck out of most kids' lives. We've got to think outside the box of what's normal, expected, and acceptable. Change won't come without a fight, but *change must come.*

Break Out of Sub-normal!

When we settle for less than what the Bible tells us to expect from our kids, and then some outstanding children cross our paths, we shake our heads and think, "That's odd." You see, when we've lived in the *subnormal* for so long and then the normal shows up, it appears to be *abnormal*. When we've lived according to *Parenting Today, American Baby,* and *Child* magazines for so long and the normal according-to-God shows up, a collision occurs in our minds. Our perceptions are challenged.

> . . . when we've lived in the *subnormal* for so long and then the normal shows up, it appears to be *abnormal.*

Isaiah 55:8 describes how our fleshly man's first response is not God's: *"For My thoughts are not your thoughts, neither are your ways My ways, declares the Lord."* Our traditions, upbringing, life experience, and previous training have produced the perceptions that feel like reality to us. Often, we've got to undo our past to go into our future.

It's imperative that we embrace the mind of Christ by the power of the Holy Spirit! 1 Corinthians 2:16 teaches us to undo wrong mind-sets. *"For who has known the mind of the Lord that he may instruct him?"* But we have the mind of *Christ.* At any point in our lives where we've believed a lie—what our culture has taught us that is contrary to what our Bible teaches—we must allow the truth of God's Word to come in, expose the lie, and undo what we've believed.

If we mean business and we're truly candidates for change, we need to allow God to crash into our perceptions. Be prepared, He may come through the door of offense. Look in the New Testament as Jesus moved about communities, just being who He was. His ideas often cut right across the preferences of so many with whom He came into contact. Offense can often become the door of revelation—and *revolution*—to us, if we'll embrace it.

At times when God wants to reveal something to me that's going to *shift my paradigm,* it can make me angry. When I'm offended, what needs to change in me is revealed. I've found that God offends my mind in order to reveal what's in my heart. Romans 3:4 urges us to *Let God be true and every man a liar.* Would you be willing to give up your opinions if you found them contrary to God's best for you and your children? A good friend of mine likes to say, "We've got to *give up to go up!*" Are you willing to give up your preferences, traditions, ruts, and biases to go up to a higher place in your home, with your children?! Will you sign up for such a challenge?

We Need a Revolution in Education

Our educational system is trying to drive our homes. It's trying to hold our kids hostage. One local Christian school's advertisement proclaims, "The only place your child spends more time than in school, is in his bed, sleeping." Not my kid.

I began to check out a private school as a possible option for one of my sons. The staff person explained that the normal homework load was two to three hours a night Monday through Friday with some on weekends. He assured me this still leaves students plenty of time to pursue their passions and have family time. Okay, I'm doing the math: he gets on the bus at 7:30 in the morning, gets home at 4:30 in the afternoon, and then has two to three hours of homework (which means four to five hours with distractions and fatigue). Add to that piano lessons, chores, church meetings, and extra-curricular activities and there's not much oxygen left in the day. Maybe by midnight we could see him again! "Thank you, but no thank you."

It's no secret that America's public educational system needs an overhaul. In my opinion, it needs a revolution, but I don't have time to wait for that to happen. I have five sons. By the time a revolution takes place in the current educational system, my kids will likely have grandkids! Since my husband and I can't depend on the government educational system to develop the potential that God has placed within our children, we've had to implement our own revolution by creating a customized system of education for our kids' sakes.

> Our educational system is trying to drive our homes. It's trying to hold our kids hostage.

By living outside the box offered us by the local public and private institutions of education, we've found freedom and success in what is often referred to as "home schooling." It's been a bumpy and lonely road at times over these nearly twenty years, but it's been the right path for our family to travel. One step has always led to the next, even when it seemed like we'd hit the wall. As pioneers, we've blazed trails until they've crossed and connected with those that others have opened up before us. I've watched the home schooling movement graduate over the years from anonymous and nearly scandalous to highly respected and recognized in many circles. For us and many other families across the earth, home schooling has proved to be an excellent solution to the education dilemma.

Even if you don't choose to home school, I believe home is still the place where your child must be taught the most important lessons of life. As parents we must make educational and extracurricular choices which allow us to have *time at home* with our children. I believe the home is the optimum place for our diamonds-in-the-rough to be polished, and we parent-teachers are best able to perfect their brilliance. Yes, I said *brilliance!* I *know* that every single one of my kids is brilliant. I know that each of your kids is brilliant too, but you might not know it yet.

John Taylor Gatto knows the brilliance within every child. Gatto taught in the public schools for twenty-six years and was named New York State Teacher of the Year in 1990. He levels the playing field of educational labels by saying, "During [these 26 years], *I've come to believe that genius is an exceedingly common human quality,* probably natural to most of us. . . . The unlikeliest kids kept demonstrating to me at random moments so many of the hallmarks of human excellence—insight, wisdom, justice, resourcefulness, courage, originality."[1]

From "Advanced" to "Slow," harmful tags put on our kids by the system instill in them a hierarchical mind-set. "Made in God's Image" is the only tag our children need to reaffirm their brilliance! It may not be brilliance for algebra, but it may be brilliance for multiplying finances into the kingdom of God, helping the poor, and loving the orphan. It may not be brilliance for spelling, but perhaps it's brilliance for winning the lost and shepherding hundreds and thousands to the Lord. Let's endeavor every day to make our homes into learning environments where our children will uniquely flourish in the giftings God has given them.

It's apparent that our traditional systems of education are broken at best and disastrous at worst. We as parents must decide if these worn and broken systems are going to wear down and break our kids. If so, it may be time for major change.

We Need a Revolution at Church

In contemporary culture, what is the number-one question of many parents visiting a church? "What do you have for our kids?" If I take out my decoder ring, this translates into, "How do you plan to entertain and baby-sit our children so we can enjoy the church meeting?" I (perhaps a bit mischievously!) want to turn and say, "How do *you* plan to train *your* children for the kingdom of God the other 166 hours you have left this week?" I'm troubled by the trend I see in parenting within the church. It seems we are preoccupied with entertaining our children.

> I'm troubled by the trend I see in parenting within the church. It seems we are preoccupied with entertaining our children.

For how many years will we continue to arrange Funland for our children, while immunizing them to true godliness and teaching them to "check out" mentally as all of

---

[1] Gatto, John T. Dumbing Us Down. (Philadelphia: New Society Publishers, 1992), p. xi.

us big people do the *real thing?* Will we push the magic button when they turn eighteen and suddenly have powerful apostolic and prophetic young men and women to carry the baton into the future? Are these entertainment junkies going to have shoulders big enough to carry the weight of all for which we're laboring? Will these over-dressed, over-fed, over-indulged little people have the character to bring this great task to fruition? I'm afraid we have erred in our thinking and will face certain peril if we don't make some radical adjustments.

The church at large appears to lack the seed of a Moses-type deliverer. I don't really perceive much difference between what the church and what secular society produce in their followers. I'm seeing the same miniskirts, the same greedy hearts, the same media addiction, the same reckless abandon with the tongue, the same disrespect toward adults, and the same eating habits of junk-food junkies. I want to see the Daniels. I want to see the Davids and the Samuels; the Deborahs and the Esthers. This standard is from the Word of God, and I believe it must impact the

> **We've got to be willing to live counter-*church*-culture, if necessary.**

church community before it can impact the world! We must be willing to take a stand in the midst of our church-going friends and peers. We've got to be willing to live counter-*church*-culture, if necessary.

Somehow I just can't see Jesus stopping to "release the children" to their classrooms before He began His Sermon on the Mount. Let's inspect our children's ministries. Let's make sure we aren't teaching our kids to tune out at every prayer meeting and worship time or during any substantial message and prophetic word that is delivered. Let's expect more and begin to ask God how the New Testament model and values we're committed to can be applied practically to our children in the local body of Christ. Let's be sure we're not "dismissing the children" when we are dismissing the children.

The state of children in our nation's churches is a festering wound. It's a potentially fatal wound if we don't turn it around. I don't care if we become a 10,000 member mega church; if our kids are not being equipped to change the world around them, then we are simply an entertainment center. I don't care how many little darlings in their tight jeans and how many guys with their cool bed-heads line up in the front of auditoriums to jump and shout to God. If there is no substance in their lives, they are just another subculture taking up space and wasting time. If there isn't something in their core beliefs which differs from the majority and expresses itself beyond the four walls of the church to bring change *out there,* then where's the beef? If they aren't living beyond their new car and their polished nails and their tanning booths by caring about the weak, loving the poor, and giving up wages for somebody else, then I have real difficulty seeing the kingdom of God in them.

The Great Generational Divide in the Local Church

Many parents think that the church is preparing their kids to understand, embrace, and walk out Christianity, but they may be dead wrong. Sometimes the methods of our local churches are detrimental to "training a child in the way he should go." *It is incumbent upon the local church leaders to assimilate our children into the mix and help them and those around them to understand that they are a vital part of the team.* We better not leave our kids in the dust and train them that they just can't handle the big stuff—stuff that God has reserved for adults only. Are we expecting that mystically—at a mysteriously right time of maturity—our kids will respond to "the call?" We must first respond to the call and then take our children with us!

> **We thinking, intelligent adults demand fresh bread for ourselves, while feeding the children stale religious fodder.**

Friends, I'm concerned that we aren't including our children in our mandate as we should. In Hosea, when a solemn fast was called, the kids were included. They weren't coloring pictures in a back room. I fear we are disqualifying our own children. We thinking, intelligent adults demand fresh bread for ourselves, while feeding the children stale religious fodder. What will be our end if we don't adjust our thinking and take action?

Many folks want to go to a church with all the bells and whistles and where Sammy puppet will jump out and tell the children not to sin. Well, let me tell you, the puppets will not come singing to Junior when the world starts pulling him down toward the sewers of life. You've got to base your choice of local church commitment on more important factors. Personally, I don't think you should choose a church based on whether "Junior has friends there" or leave a church because "nobody his age is there." You better take him to a church that is building on the right foundations, so that when Junior is fifteen, he'll have some solid spiritual bedrock upon which to stand.

I'm not against excellence and creativity in our children's ministries, but I am against entertaining our future leaders at the expense of training them biblically. Will they have a theology strong enough to serve as their foundation for withstanding the storms on the horizon? Will they know how to rightly divide the Word of truth when they've spent so many years eating cookies in back rooms?

Are we building pillars that will stand in the temple or reeds shaking in the wind? We must turn the tide. In Luke 18:16, *Jesus called the children to him and said, "Let the little children come to me, and do not hinder them . . ."* In order to keep things tidy and acceptable in our meetings, are we sterilizing the growth quotient of our youngsters?

The Bible—just as it is—provides acceptable reading material for our children. We wonder why our kids can only handle milk and not meat? Because we've stuck a bottle in their mouths to keep them quiet for so long that they haven't developed teeth. They choke and cough and complain if there isn't mirth in everything that takes place. Peril approaching! All is not well! We need a revolution in our kids' ministries!

As Christians, we're facing desperate days which call for desperate measures on all fronts: the family, the school, and the church. It's time for strong leaders—militant, believing, devout adults and children—to march forward and bring about revolutionary change in a dying world.

CHAPTER THREE

Anybody Home?

The most important work you and I will ever do will be within the walls of our own homes.

—Harold B. Lee

Far too many children in America and in other westernized nations of the earth do not have the attention of their parents. We are a distracted people who want to pay someone else to engage our children. Parenting takes precious time. Preoccupied parents cannot fulfill the high calling of directing their child to his destiny. So many moms and dads are checked-out while little Junior has license to run his own life. We're looking the other way as he's stealing the farm! He holds the reins of his young life, with a full menu of web browsers, video games, stereos, telephones, and televisions at his disposal. Little does he know, enemies are lurking all around.

We know one young man of fifteen who drives himself, at his whim, wherever and whenever he desires in the family car. It is conveniently parked outside the empty, over-sized house in which everyone sleeps but does not otherwise live. What a tragedy to see the multitudes of wealthy orphans in our cities, unequipped to deal wisely with the innumerable freedoms handed to them at such indiscriminate ages. Millions of clueless youngsters are raising themselves. What sacred destinies have been placed in their unscrupulous hands!

Many children in our nation represent a new brand of orphan. They may sleep in designer bed sheets, but their lonely hearts pine for their disengaged parents. These ten-year-old, free moral agents live on the edge of destruction, wearing the latest fashions and never lacking cash while surviving their impoverished family lives. These orphans are in your neighborhood, and you may not even notice them: minors left for 12 and 14 hours a day with nobody looking after them. One such story relating to this issue comes to mind.

Greeley, Colorado: Here's a case of a real-life *Home Alone* minus Macaulay Culkin. A mother from Greeley, Colorado, skipped off to Italy leaving her six children, aged six to fourteen, to fend for themselves with only a credit card and $7 in cash (*Wireless Flash*, February 17, 2003). At the time the story ran, this mother was still at large somewhere in Italy with her boyfriend.

The media hypocritically reported this incident of abandonment as an unusual and scandalous crime, while day after day ignoring our modern plague in the U.S.: masses of kids commonly home alone in our cities for extended periods of time. Those who do decry the calamity of latch-key kids but relentlessly endorse the working-mother lifestyle as worthwhile and noble should be ashamed of their double standards.

Who's minding the children and guiding their habits? Who's monitoring their media intake and building in prized values? Who's nagging them like all good mothers and fathers should? Galatians 4:19 calls us to this passionate burden: *My dear children for whom I am again in the pains of childbirth until Christ is formed in you.* Physical labor at childbirth is a piece of cake compared to the seemingly infinite, ensuing labors that take place in prayer and in person with and for our children to become Christ-like. Effective, biblical parenting can be exhausting! It involves *wrestling* opposition to the ground, first by prayer then by counsel, correction, exhortation, encouragement, argument, theology, and whatever other means are required to bring our children into a realization and understanding of the lordship of Jesus Christ in their everyday lives.

> **Who's minding the children and guiding their habits?**

Let's be unwilling to allow others to raise our children. Let's not be so quick to turn our dearest treasures over to those who haven't birthed them. Someone must nurture the children. Someone must mold the soft clay of their hearts and minds. Someone must be the constant for these tender humans in the midst of a chaotic world. Someone must be the anchor for their souls in this turbulent time. Our hearts must cry out, "Oh God, give us mothers and fathers once again."

Parents' Spheres of Influence

This revelation will change your life: *As a mom or dad operating in your God-given role as a parent, you are the most powerful person in the world in that sphere. A God-given role is a function that no one else has the capacity to fill. It's uniquely ours to maintain and protect and develop to its highest possibility.* Talk about superheroes! Only we have the authority to fully employ all of our resources, both human and material, to impart and impose our vision upon our sphere and, in so doing, get the job done. 1 Corinthians 4:2 urges, *Now it is required that those who have been given a trust [sphere] must prove faithful.*

The most common criminal act today is parents who prove unfaithful in their sphere. No, folks won't dial 911 when a parent abandons his or her post. It won't be reported in the local newspaper, and it's unlikely that the parents will be jailed or even taken to the county courthouse to stand trial. Nevertheless, I call it criminal behavior, right up there with robbery, arson, and manslaughter.

"Denise, you are making some dramatic statements, aren't you?" one might ask. My friends, I'm seeing tragic, dramatic results from this pattern of life, and it's going to take severe adjustments on our part if we want our society to prosper as in days gone by.

Let me illustrate. Babies are born in House A and in House B.

- **In House A**, Mom and Dad enjoy baby for six weeks with Mom home on leave from her career. Before they know it, it's time for Mom to go back to work, place baby in childcare, and continue pursuing her meaningful and gainful employment. After all, diapers get old, and all that stuff isn't very glamorous compared to moving on the fast track of upward mobility. Or, perhaps Dad doesn't see value in Mom's being home with baby and insists she generate income.

Every situation cannot be painted with one, broad brush, so please hear my heart. There are many and varied circumstances. I don't want to bring condemnation to those who find themselves currently dependent on others for their child's daily care, yet we must come into the full realization of what sin and our choices are doing to the next generation.

In our broken world, countless women have been abandoned, abused, or widowed and find themselves living with the ominous task of caring for their children as a single parent for at least a season. Men, too, have been deserted and left to bear the weight of raising kids on their own. Hear me well: *God's grace is sufficient!* (2 Corinthians 12:9). He is still a father to the fatherless and a defender of widows (Psalms 68:5). Whatever the case, Mom has been taken out of her God-given sphere of motherhood. The responsibility, joy, and privilege of nurturing her baby and managing his young life has been handed over to someone else for most of this little one's waking hours.

- **House B** is astir due to the arrival of a new little one. Mom has always worked outside the home, but when she and Dad face the reality of her leaving Baby B, they're overcome with grief and a sense of loss. As Dad looks into the face of baby, he realizes childcare is out of the question. Their life takes on some major changes. Mom finds herself lingering over B in the morning, praying for God to do big things for this tiny creature. Singing over him, she senses the voice of God whispering in her ear about his destiny. She is captivated by this child.

As he grows, her prayers grow, taking on more shape and more detail concerning his future. The time to train him draws near. She and Dad are gripped with a powerful urge to direct him properly and discipline him according to the Word. They see such promise in his young face and watch his giftings unfold, even in their rudimentary stages.

Mom begins investing the lion's share of her resources into this sphere called home. She develops her skills as a wife and mother. She learns to manage her growing household. Now, without the formidable eight-hour workday with a two-hour commute, she suddenly finds substantial time for local church involvement and deepening relationships in the body of Christ. Her life becomes driven by her goal of living out the kingdom of God and raising her young disciple who will one day change the world.

This child is hugely and positively impacted by a mother and father who are actively and radically praying, working, nurturing, training, and getting their hands around every aspect of that baby's life. It is beautiful to watch. These invested parents offer the kind of stuff that no day care can emulate. Eternal purpose is unfolding before their eyes and the eyes of those who observe them. This is power: parents in their very own home directing a little human being into his highest purpose for life.

> **This is power: parents in their very own home directing a little human being into his highest purpose for life.**

Unlimited potential can be unlocked by the humble hands of a mother and father who team up in this, their God-given sphere. We must not abandon our spheres! No one else can raise our children. No one can do it better than we can. We have been given this charge by Almighty God! What more can be said? Dare we pawn off this responsibility to some cheap replacement? Dare we settle for mediocre substitutes when we are the experts on our own children? What are we thinking, imagining that this holy task can be hired out to others? It is insanity.

What is so heinous about this crime of the away-from-home, working-mom culture? It is the pitiful fruit of weak, twisted, and underdeveloped children and young adults in America and other first-world countries of the earth. Countless paltry, rebellious, cynical, and lazy specimens called "youth" are the fruit of parents abandoning their chief sphere in favor of far less important pursuits of career, financial success, status, love of pleasure, material possessions, and entertainment. Let us highly resolve to give the devil back his toys and run like crazy back to our spheres, where true success—eternal treasure—awaits our investment.

The Practicalities of Proactive Parenting

Walking out the reality of such a resolution is not rocket science, but it will require prodigious effort in practical matters. When a father and mother decide to take back their God-given injunction to subdue and rule over the earth, they must realize that such dominion begins in the home. They set their alarms an hour early to rise and seek God, read His Word, and spend time praying earnestly for Junior and little Susie. They look over the calendar and realize there is only one evening a week with nothing planned. They pick up the phone and begin to cancel two out of the four regular extra-curricular activities which are proving to be time wasters and people pleasers.

These determined parents take time to lay hands on their children, praying over them and imparting the good things of God each day. During breakfast, Dad or Mom shares a segment of Scripture, applies it to their children's lives, and urges the children to serve the living God. Mom and Dad together begin to see the special qualities God has given their children and make efforts to encourage them in these aspects of their character.

Dad calls and cancels the cable television service which seems to devour hours of valuable time while bringing unsavory elements into the home. He installs software on the computer to ensure the kids are protected from dangerous predators as they log on to use the web. Mom and Dad now use an internet service to screen all movies with questionable content before their children are allowed to view them. They stand guard vigorously at the gate of their home, unwilling to bend to the evil influences beckoning.

Mom begins to clean out the cupboards, realizing all the processed garbage, erroneously labeled "food," has to go in favor of homemade soups and big lively salads with grainy breads. She decides that kids *can* drink water after all. The cookie jar is stored up and away and fresh fruit decorates the kitchen. Dad unplugs the phone at dinner time, so they can actually breathe and hear each other talk during the meal.

I promise you, this household will never be the same once these parents begin to take back the ground that is theirs to maintain, develop, and cause to flourish. So many are waiting for God to "work their land" when God has given *us* that job. Proverbs 28:19 clearly states, *He who works his land will have abundant food, but the one who chases fantasies will have his fill of poverty*. We must do that which we are called by God to do, and He will do the rest.

Childcare Institutions

Almost everyday, I drive by a familiar yellow house on the east side of a main road near my home. It's recently been converted into a childcare center. More often than not, there is a "Help Wanted" sign posted out front near the street. I imagine the average person drives by unaffected by such a common plea in our culture. Not me.

The location of this sign is what haunts me. I ponder these vulnerable little people being dropped off for the day. I can see them, wide-eyed, looking up into alien faces every few weeks after a new hiring has taken place. They begin their long day of childcare perhaps a bit uneasy, a knot in their stomach, a sense that all is not well. They're no longer in friendly waters, but find themselves over their heads emotionally, trying to work out in their minds, "Who is this stranger and where is Bonnie, the smiling lady with brown hair who used to open the door?"

As I consider these vulnerable youngsters, the transient nature of childcare centers is enough to break my heart. But I can't blame the employees. They haven't been equipped to carry such a mammoth weight—mothering children with whom they have no real relationship or in whom they have no real interest.

I have close friends who own and run three of the finest day care centers in our city. They are providing an unusually positive option in the childcare world. They've made the best of a bad situation for parents who don't have time or don't make time to rear their young. However, they too face the dilemma of employee burnout from time to time. Several gals from our church work at these day cares, and one of the girls came to this conclusion: The reason childcare workers burn out is because it's completely unnatural to raise another's sons and daughters. It is not their sphere, so it will never work out long-term. Inevitably, employees will wear down, quit, and move on.

> **It's up to us Moms and Dads to decide who the heroes will be for our sons and daughters.**

The majority of day care settings employ a mass system of herding youngsters like animals with a one-size-fits-all method, which should be unthinkable to a rational parent. How can we turn our sons and daughters over to complete strangers? Loan out your personal stuff with reckless abandon, but hold those little ones close to your heart. Most Americans wouldn't trust even a close friend with their checkbook or pin numbers, but we'll trust our children to just about anyone.

If my child were in day care, dismal questions would weigh on my mind: Whose hands will touch my son on Thursday? Where have those hands been, and are they gentle, pure hands? What compromises will take place due to shorthanded staff or human weakness? Whose image will Junior bear at the end of his season at Kiddieland? Whose morals, heart, tendencies, and habits will Susie emulate? It's up to us Moms and Dads to decide who the heroes will be for our sons and daughters. We must carefully choose the handprints left on our offspring.

I look into the hollow eyes of many a child locked away in day care settings most of their waking hours. Their substance is being formed, and their character is being fashioned. Their "wet cement" is being set by foreign hands and contrary hearts, day in and day out. Later, around adolescence, these same children may have few distinctive markings or admirable qualities. I see young men and women formed in the manner of a societal assembly line of Egypt. Oh, how quickly the years go by! Children slam the door of childhood with their own hands, pursuing popularity and romance among their peer group of scrawny, fellow prisoners of the system. Where are the major players, Mom and Dad? Let's take a look.

CHAPTER FOUR

Where's Dad?

Dad is destiny. More than virtually any other factor, a biological father's presence in the family will determine a child's success and happiness.

—*U.S. News and World Report*
February 27, 1995

Proverbs 4, 5, 6, and 7 record a letter from a father to a son. Take time to read through and ponder its contents. It will amaze you. This is not only a practical road map for success in life, but also an impassioned, urgent plea for the very soul of this young man. These weighty words of life from the sincere and thoughtful heart of a hands-on, engaged father begin with an urgent, *"Listen to what I say!"*

I want to ask you, Dad, what are *you* saying to your son or daughter? "Rams beat the Broncos 21–14 on Sunday." Or, "What's for dinner?" How 'bout, "Gimme a beer and put on the game!" Maybe, "Who turned the darn thermostat so high?" Or even, "Where is my hammer?!" Is this the extent of your profound interaction?

If that's the best you can do, then should your son be hearing what you have to say? Would *anyone* want to hear what comes out of your mouth? So many dads seem relegated only to grunting and eating meals with the family. There is so much more ground to be taken by fathers! There is a rich, divine inheritance waiting to be tapped.

Note how Samson's father responded to the angel of God upon hearing the good news of his wife's pregnancy after a long period of infertility. Judges 13:12 says, *So Manoah [Samson's father] asked him, "When your words are fulfilled, what is to be the rule for the boy's life and work?"* Samson's father inquired seriously of the Lord about raising his son.

This dad didn't mess with the trifle of building a bassinette. He was preoccupied with building a man of God even before his birth! With many living with the disappointment of infertility in our day, most fathers would celebrate the news of a miraculous conception with friends and a couple of beers. They would be ecstatic to see the test strip turn purple, but their last thought would be, "How can I prepare to properly train him?"

It's time for fathers to take back the reigns of fatherhood, not by pounding their fists and arrogantly declaring they are rulers of their homes, but by being servant leaders to their families. Dads, you have got to put that cloth over your arm, take up the wash basin that Jesus used, and become what you must become for your sons and daughters.

You aren't called to be king of the hill, but you are called to be the king and priest of your home in a closet where nobody sees you. How many times do your kids run into the room to find the remote going . . . Dad surfing channels . . . checking out? How often do your kids bump into you on your knees? How many times, Dad, does your son or daughter catch you not eating that day because you're crying out to God with fasting and prayer?

It should happen hundreds of times during your children's growing-up years. They come into the room and find Mom or Dad on their knees. Mom is here, or Dad is there with the Word of God open. What are we doing? Are we just opening our Bibles once or twice a week, maybe on Sunday? Stop! Think! That is not Christianity. If that's how we're living, then we aren't building anything. We must tear down that mentality. It's a lie. We're just decorating our lives with religion.

Mighty Weapons in Our Hands

Psalms 127:4–5 says, *Like arrows in the hands of a warrior are sons born in one's youth. Blessed is the man whose quiver is full of them. They will not be put to shame when they contend with their enemies in the gate.*

Dads, you've got to get the revelation that the rambunctious children crawling, toddling, and racing through the rooms of your house aren't just kids, they're *weapons*, and they come to you with great responsibility. I have to ask you men, "Where are you and what are you doing with your arrows? Are you living by the light of your computers, driven by e-mails and briefcases? Is it always the cell phone, the newspaper, and the television that occupy your hours at home? Have you relegated this task of arrow-refining to the little woman?"

> I have to ask you men, "Where are you and what are you doing with your arrows?"

"What's so great about an arrow?" one might ask. An arrow doesn't sound like much until you remember back in Bible days there weren't guns, bombs, and missiles. Think slings, catapults, and battering rams! Thus, the Bible says a man was blessed who had *arrows*: weapons of precision, speed, and power. A good arrow was a marvelous asset to a man in those days.

- **Arrows are meant to penetrate.** If our arrow-sons and daughters are going to kill or put the enemy to flight, they must be sharp. A blunt arrow is pretty worthless unless you want to swing it at someone and hope you don't miss. How sharp will your arrows be? Who will sharpen your arrows to a point of truth that penetrates the darkness?
- **An arrow must have impetus.** Impetus is the force which drives an arrow forward *against resistance*. Disengaged dads can't give children the impetus they need to resist the ever-present powers of darkness intent upon their downfall. Without impetus, our arrow-children won't go far enough from the quiver to be noticed by angels or demons.
- **The velocity at which an arrow is set in motion will determine its force of impact.** Without speed, an arrow won't hit anything but the archer's toe! Who will help your child set the velocity at which he builds the kingdom of God on earth? Who will ensure that your arrow isn't spiritually sluggish? As your child's role model, are you swift and vigorous as you follow God and seek to fulfill His purposes in the earth?
- **Lastly, aim is of the utmost importance!** Neglecting to give our arrow-child clear direction is to cause him to miss the target! We mustn't neglect our *daily* job of pointing our arrow accurately in order to see it hit the mark for God's kingdom.

We as parents are to propel our children as arrows toward a mark of greatness. We dare not drop these potentially powerful weapons along the path of least resistance, dooming them to lives of normalcy. Let God plant a lasting seed of desire in your heart to raise godly leaders and to turn them loose as effective arrows, penetrating the pockets of darkness in the earth.

> **We as parents are to propel our children as arrows toward a mark of greatness.**

Threatened by Extinction

Environmental issues are hot topics these days. A newscast wouldn't be complete without hearing about the latest efforts of organizations like Greenpeace and Defenders of Wildlife. Their heroic attempts to save Old McDonald's Farm and all its relations from extinction have forced the world to take notice and make changes. Extinction is the disappearance, brought about by natural or unnatural means, of an *entire species*.

I love the starfish, sand dollar, and harbor seal which are native to our Pacific Northwest region, and I take seriously the charge to live responsibly in order that succeeding generations will continue enjoying these sea creatures. But I take far more seriously a threatened extinction of a different sort, the disappearance of the significant, God-ordained role of *fathers* in our day. It seems fatherhood has evolved until it's barely recognizable in scores of families today. When we put our finger on Dad's pulse, it grows fainter each moment.

Careful examination of Pop's involvement in the lives of his children reveals a troubling trend in America. It seems his customary place at the head of our dinner tables is vanishing. Consider the fact that nearly two of every five kids do not live with their dads. That amounts to an astonishing 38 percent of all kids who now live without their biological fathers—up from just 17.5 percent in 1960. These stats may not take your breath away until you realize the ramifications of this abnormal shift.

Did you know that 46 percent of families with children headed by single mothers live below the poverty line, compared with eight percent of those with two parents? Sociologists Sara McLanahan and Gary Sandefur say in their book, *Growing Up With a Single Parent*, that young women who were reared in disrupted families are *twice* as likely to become teen mothers.[2]

Social scientists have made similar links between a father's absence and his child's likelihood to be a dropout, drug addict, suicide victim, target of childhood sexual abuse, as well as one who suffers from mental illness or unemployment. Consider that 70 percent of the two million men incarcerated in United States' prisons never had a relationship with their natural father. It appears from these findings that Dad indeed

> **...Dad indeed determines destiny.**

determines destiny, and he, apart from any other factor aside from Almighty God, could be holding the key to the tomorrows of not only America, but the nations of the earth (*U.S. News and World Report,* February 27, 1995).

"'Fatherless-ness' is the most destructive trend of our generation," argues David Blankenhorn, author of *Fatherless America: Confronting Our Most Urgent Social Problem.* Such a statement is understandable when surveying the damage incurred by default dads. Short of radical change, our future as a nation doesn't appear to be glowing brightly when you face the fact that 68 percent of black children and 30 percent of all kids in America are being born outside of marriage (*U.S. News and World Report, February 27, 1995*).

---

[2] McLanahan & Sandefur. *Growing Up with a Single Parent* (Harvard University Press, 2006).

Bear in mind, these bleak findings weren't researched and analyzed by overly enthusiastic born-again Christians. This was a secular study eyeballing the hard facts. Based on these findings in America, it's not hard to connect the dots of our social ills across the entire earth and see how Dad's role is paramount in the healthy development of not only *his* children, but in turn, *entire cities!*

Dad-Quakes!

Dad not only determines the fate of his own family, but the impact from his choices in fathering for good or bad will be felt like an earthquake, reverberating out his front door and into the streets of our communities. At this very moment across the globe, our youngest and most innocent are experiencing relentless tremors day after agonizing day from the effects of their own dad-induced earthquakes. According to these studies and apart from the grace of God, their personal catastrophes will in turn bring seismic repercussions of enormous proportion, affecting our neighborhoods, our businesses, our schools, our lives, and our nations. I'm reminded of Carole King's 1972 classic, "*I Feel the Earth Move.*"[3]

I know I'm feeling the earth move under my feet here in Seattle due to the aftershock of rampant fatherless-ness. I know the sky is tumblin' down—a tumblin' down for millions of fatherless children in every city across the globe, and it's bringing our local church body to their knees. Week after week we're crying out in prayer for God to do what no man can do. May the body of Christ across the earth be a symphony of voices pleading for this miracle before the throne of Almighty God day and night, giving Him no rest until we see the fulfillment of this promise from Malachi 4:6: *He will turn the hearts of the fathers to their children, and the hearts of the children to their fathers; or else I will come and strike the land with a curse.* One peek at this data, and we know we are living under a divine curse on the earth.

The ongoing accumulation of rubble from the war on fatherhood is mind boggling. Under normal circumstances, a natural disaster of this magnitude would merit assistance from the National Guard, the Red Cross, anyone! It would be front-page news for weeks on end. Donations would pour in, and relief would be realized for the hurting victims. But this is war of a different kind, and countless children are finding no relief from being abandoned by their fathers. Life goes marching on without missing a beat, and newscast after newscast plays out with no mention of this devastation in home after home after home.

---

[3] King, Carole. *I Feel the Earth Move* (Tapestry. Epic, 1999).

Change Is Coming!

As long as there is life, there is hope. I believe we are going to see twenty, thirty, forty, fifty, and sixty-year-old dads suddenly awakened by the Holy Spirit to become the fathers they haven't been for the glory of God. *It's not too late*, even for grandfathers to realize their power to lead in the lives of their children and grandchildren. Imagine, even now, that your phone rings. At the other end of the line is your grandpa, hem-hawing awkwardly, trying to begin a conversation with you—perhaps the first one you've had in years. He mumbles something about wanting to take you and the kids to the lake for a week of fun and to catch up on life together. He's sending a check to cover your expenses and making sure the dates will work for you.

As you pick yourself up off the floor, you think you heard him say, "Been praying for you all," and you're back on the floor! I believe we're going to see some unusual, wonderful results as men begin to take the lead in restoring relationships long ago abandoned. Men in prisons are going to begin *writing* letters to their children; men in prisons are going to begin *receiving* letters from their fathers. We are going to see a revolution take place in the arena of fathering. Which one of us can resist a father who has come to his senses? Which one of us could tell Grandpa to "get lost" when he's making servant-hearted advances to breech the wall of separation that has existed for decades?

> **In my opinion, a father carries an authority that is intrinsic.**

If restoration to a natural father is impossible, I believe we'll see men of all ages become fathers to children not biologically theirs. My own sons, at their young ages, are actively fathering even men who are their seniors. This is the work of God. Sons and daughters are waiting for you, men of God. So many are fatherless in our day, longing for the leadership only a man can bring. Will you volunteer to father even those not descended of your natural flesh and blood? I believe many will. Our prayers will not go unanswered. James 5:16 reminds us that *The prayer of a righteous man is powerful and effective.*

In my opinion, a father carries an authority that is intrinsic. There is a commanding influence with which God has equipped Dad for the immense role he is to play in the life of his family. When Dad finally speaks, there is power. Dad, don't settle for merely built-in clout, but take advantage of your God-given assets and wildly enhance them with all of your strength and passion as you move toward the children God has given you. Be the world-changer you are called

> **When Dad finally speaks, there is power.**

to be, and your children will sky-rocket from your broad shoulders of strong leadership into the galaxies beyond.

This passage from Isaiah will become yours. *Lift up your eyes and look about you: All assemble and come to you; your sons come from afar, and your daughters are carried on the arm. Then you will look and be radiant, your heart will throb and swell with joy; the wealth on the seas will be brought to you, to you the riches of the nations will come (Isaiah 60:4–5). No greater joy could be ours than to know our sons and daughters are walking in the truth (3 John 1:4)!*

CHAPTER FIVE

Where's Mom?

I learned more about Christianity from my mother than from all the theologians of England.

—John Wesley

It is often a rich child who sits in a poor mother's lap.

—Danish Proverb

A common modern "dilemma" now faces every pregnant woman: Whatever shall we do after the baby is born? Why are we Christians asking the same questions that the lost women of this world are asking? Why do I see "miracle babies" being born to seemingly barren women in the church and then find the baby is being raised by someone else in a day care? Just as in the days of Moses, when the evil king's decree stood supreme, it seems that today's ruling decree mandates, "Day care is acceptable and *expected* for Junior."

Mom, defy this trend! Reject this world's decrees. Resolve to live within your husband's paycheck. Sell the second car and the house if necessary. We must take serious measures to flourish in treacherous times. Let's set a new trend. Believe God to meet you at your point of faith, even though it doesn't seem feasible. Make the necessary adjustments and watch God move!

The following quote has impacted my life since the day I heard it. W.H. Murray certainly understands faith when he explains, "The moment one definitely *commits oneself*, then Providence moves too. All sorts of things occur to help that would never otherwise have occurred. A stream of events issues from the decision, raising unforeseen incidents

> **One resolute and unbending decision is a powerful force.**

and meetings and material assistance, which no man could have dreamt would have come his way. I have learned a deep respect for one of Goethe's couplets: 'What you can do, or dream you can, *begin it*. Boldness has genius, power and magic in it.'" I agree!

One resolute and unbending decision is a powerful force. A single-minded commitment to the principles which God is speaking regarding your childrearing will topple one circumstantial domino after another, finally bringing you to the fulfillment of the vision God has given you.

At this holy moment when a difficult decision toward righteousness is made by faith, even though nothing has changed in the natural, everything is different in the spiritual realm! You haven't won the lottery; you're still living in the same overpriced home; your two new cars and the RV are still sitting outside in the drive; and your inflated Visa bill just arrived in the mail. But decisions to begin to change are pivotal because you are now postured intently toward ruthless obedience. You are ready to do anything God asks of you concerning your kingdom home and family. Therefore, everything has changed. If this describes you, it's time to take decisive, disciplined steps in your parenting such as:

- living on your knees for your children's destinies
- seeking guidance from God in your parenting skills with a humble and teachable heart
- slashing the budget to keep Mom at home for child training
- embracing kingdom priorities as the purpose and force that drive your life

These are the earmarks of a parent who is poised and ready!

Busy at Home

I've decided it's time to swing the pendulum back—with full force—to women being busy at home. I'm sick to death of walking into all manner of businesses and seeing young women shackled to a desk for forty-plus hours a week, while nearby photos of their children falsely comfort them with the lie of pseudo-mothering. Babies need their mommies. These dedicated, hard-working women are in the wrong place at the wrong time. These young mothers are hugely sacrificing, but sorely misguided. Mom suffers for it, her marriage suffers for it, her children suffer for it, but everybody in the mainstream thinks it's absolutely normal! The world cheers her on!

Once again, counter-culture is where we have to live. Titus 2:4 puts it clearly enough: *Then they can train the younger women to love their husbands and children, to be self-*

controlled and pure, to be busy at home. Women, first things first! The world is waiting for our greatness, but it's not out there in the marketplace in this season of childrearing.

We mothers must find contentment in our calling as mothers. The lure to work outside the home is strong, appealing, and seemingly liberating. I recently sat on an airplane headed to San Francisco amidst a lively group of apparently successful office chums. The discussions were flying—pardon the pun—and filled with healthy office banter. All the buzz about position and status, stocks, CEOs, FPOs, and PCs was a bit dizzying. The intoxicating smell of success filled the cabin. How seductive is the sweet nectar of worldly achievement in such a moment.

The day-in and day-out monotony of breeding laundry, cranky kids, and sticky kitchen floors can wear down the best of 'em. The adrenalin rush women may feel as they move mountains in the work world among strong men who welcome their input just isn't the same sensation one feels as she wipes runny noses, manages household chaos, and patiently potty trains disinterested toddlers.

> **Women, first things first! The world is waiting for our greatness, but it's not out there in the marketplace in this season of childrearing.**

In days gone by, *mothering* was a given for *mothers.* Hmm. In our day, however, mothering is the ultimate sacrifice of our human will as independent, new-age women who can "be anything." The options our culture hands us have placed so many women in a quandary. God has given all mothers a multiplicity of giftings and abilities to use at their discretion. We can be lured into believing, however pridefully, that we are the exceptionally gifted and shouldn't waste our illustrious talents on boring household industry. The world would scream, "What a waste not to employ those gifts for personal gain!"

But we must choose to echo Paul's declaration from 1 Corinthians 15:31, *I die daily.* I die to my worldly ambitions, my former independence, my need for accolades from my peers, and anything else keeping me from becoming an exceptional, godly mother. Colossians 3:3 reminds us as Christian mothers, *For you died, and your life is now hidden with Christ in God.*

You died. What defined who you were in former days? Perhaps you were a bookkeeper, accountant, designer, lawyer, engineer, or teacher. There is value in each of these professions. However, professional titles can subtly become our identity and an illegitimate source of self-esteem. Seasons come and seasons go for us women, and they demand our flexibility and discernment. Holding on to yesterday's role out of a need for security will rob us of the rich tomorrows that God wants to give us in our new role as mothers. Whatever function we're fulfilling at the moment, whether as office workers, full-time mothers, or mothers who work part-time out of our homes, ultimately, our identity must be anchored in Jesus Christ. When this is true of us, we easily transition from season to season in God, whether single, married, childless, or childbearing.

Hidden-ness

We find ourselves in a place of hidden-ness during the season when we are in the thick of childrearing. When I was a young mother of small children, a story about David in the Old Testament came alive to me. Perhaps it will encourage you. David, a shepherd, was the youngest of eight sons born to a man named Jesse who lived in Bethlehem. God sent Samuel to their city to anoint the new king of Israel, and unbeknownst to Jesse, one of his sons was this king-to-be. While the glorious event of anointing a king was taking place, David the shepherd boy was stuck out on the lonely hills caring for the bleating sheep. *He lived a season of being unseen, while looking after the lambs.*

God actually frustrated the prophet Samuel as he was trying to figure out which son of Jesse was "the man," until Samuel asked in near-embarrassment, "Jesse, I'm struggling here because none of these seven guys is the one. You wouldn't happen to have any other sons, would you?" In 1 Samuel 16:11 we see that Samuel asked Jesse, *"Are these all the sons you have?" "There is still the youngest,"* Jesse answered, *"but he [David] is tending the sheep." Samuel said, "Send for him; we will not sit down until he arrives."* There was David, seemingly isolated on the hills with the sheep. Yet, God was there with him, promoting him day by day!

God saw every little thing that David did with his righteous character and happy heart. He chose to find contentment in his solitary circumstances with those sheep. At the time it seemed as if David was "nobody" compared to his socially abounding and handsome older brothers. But God was up to something.

Many of the Psalms, which are forever recorded in Scripture, were actually songs David sang as he was caring for these lambs. David found joy in the sacrifice of serving and kept a song in his heart! This passage gave me such encouragement when I was in the middle of diapers, nursery duty, and feeling as though I might be missing out on important stuff that was happening somewhere else.

We mothers must learn to *mine the gold* in our current circumstances and discover contentment in any state in which we find ourselves. Whether nursing our babe at 3 A.M., cleaning up spills at mealtime, or working through perpetual mountains of laundry while simultaneously cooking dinner at 5 P.M., there must be a song in our hearts! When we realize the power in our parenting, those mundane and boring tasks of childrearing become life, excitement, and possibility! If we embrace the right mind-set, there can be a sweet satisfaction in every little thing we do in our homes, for our families. If we

> **We mothers must learn to *mine the gold* in our current circumstances and discover contentment in any state in which we find ourselves.**

understand the joy of sacrifice and service as unto the Lord, then no moment is lost!

Once you have chosen the investment of sacrifice, you willingly lay down your life and die daily for the greater good—training up this child in the way he should go. In order to serve the best interests of this little one, you've chosen to give up extended periods of sleep, spontaneous evenings spent with friends, uninterrupted shopping excursions, and all the other options you took for granted for so long. Your preferences and convenient lifestyle are now sacrificed—put to death—for this little person. But that's not the end of the story. Just as the death of Jesus on the cross was not the end of the story, so also our sacrificial "death" always brings life in the kingdom scope of things. Matthew 16:25 reminds us, *For whoever wants to save his life will lose it, but whoever loses his life for me will find it.* Our death to the triviality of worldly pleasures brings life to our whole household and to us as well. Death to my obstinate flesh has no comparison to the life I've found. Saying "no" to my self-pity is a "yes" to embracing all the joys of motherhood.

Oh, the *life* I've found—the infinite joys of mothering, drinking in the sweetness of my five sons, enjoying every age, every new awakening, every middle-of-the-night nursing time, every new word learned, every funny outfit they've chosen, snuggling close to read God's Word, hearing them proclaim new discoveries as we walk hand-in-hand along spring paths . . . these are pleasures not even a queen can purchase! Every day is a party with my priceless boys—if I choose to enjoy it. God makes sure we don't miss out on anything! Cling tightly to His promises. He's preparing us mothers for wonderful things tomorrow, even as we're involved in wonderful things with our sons and daughters today.

The Power of Motherhood

I believe the best-kept secret, to the detriment of every culture on the earth today, is the power available and resident within the life of a mom. Yep, the average mother living in modern, suburban America, to the townships of Durban, South Africa, still holds in her very hands the option of *ruling the world*. Her heart, her values, her strongest beliefs and convictions about life will be imprinted upon her sons and daughters. Whether she is persuaded by passivity, greed, and injustice or by self-sacrifice, godliness, and biblical thinking, these beliefs will become flesh within the walls of her home. Minute by minute, day by day, year by year, she will model for her offspring what is of most value to her.

Long after she's gone, even over the course of multiple generations, Mom's posterity will feel the effects of what she has strongly enforced or what she left lacking in her recipe for life on this earth. How many women have courageously and aggressively led their children into the things of God, modeling a life laid down at the feet of the Master? Too many others have left a huge vacuum, teaching their children by default that at the end of the day eternity isn't all that important. Her song is: "Eat, drink and be merry . . . for tomorrow we may die!"

It is not the heads of state or CEOs of *Fortune 500* companies who write the history of our nations and drive our economies. Do not believe a lie. It is those who *shape* our nations' future leaders who hold the most power in their hands.

What could tempt me to allow myself to be deposed from my seat of highest importance? What lowly mess of pottage could woo me away from the most important job on the planet? What perks, benefits, or retirement plan could possibly tantalize me when held up to this—the privileged call of motherhood?

Mothers, let me remind you that in our homes we sit on the second-highest seat of authority under heaven, next to our husbands. We hold authority with tomorrow's parents, teachers, lawyers, apostles, prophets, evangelists, and business owners. Our richest resources are not silver and gold or the power of our fist, but our sons and daughters.

We can have lasting impact as women by being *busy at home*. What are we doing day and night? With what are we preoccupied when our primary occupation ought to be influencing the next generation? Who will leave an imprint on these little minds and shape their characters? Will it be the ever-transient staff at KiddyCare, or will it be the lady with the burgeoning day care in her home who lives conveniently nearby? Maybe Grandma? Aunt Peggy? Friends, let's get back to the Bible. There is a time when you hide those little ones. Moses' mother and father hid him for a season. Samuel was at home for a season. Samson's dad said, "How do we raise this kid?" He didn't ask, "How close by is the day care center?" We are so worldly in our thinking. As women, we must reject the lie that we can "have it all," all at once. We can have it all on the right timeline in due season, one step at a time, but not all at once.

I want us moms to give our best to those who are most valuable to us. 1 Corinthians 6:19–20 says that *you are not your own; you were bought at a price. Therefore honor God with your body.* Jesus' blood paid the price for our lives. We now belong to Him and to His purpose. His purpose is always for us to lay down our lives for others. We must echo Jesus' words in Hebrews 10:5 and 7 . . . *when Christ came into the world, he said, "Sacrifice and offering you did not desire, but a body you prepared for me . . . Here I am . . . I have come to do your will, O God."* Just like Jesus Christ, we have options, but we must choose to do the right thing, not merely the convenient or easy thing.

It isn't some huge privilege that wives now get to work just to qualify couples for that double-income house and SUV. I want to say, "Sell that sucker! Do whatever it takes to be with your children. Quit your job, Mom, and live in a tent." Just how serious are we about what we say we want to see in our children?

> **As women, we must reject the lie that we can "have it all," all at once.**

I hear young, naive mothers say, "Oh, I'm having a baby! I'm so excited! Afterward I get six weeks off and then I only have to work part-time. It's just going to be mornings." "Mornings" turn into three o'clock in the afternoon. You might as well kiss the day goodbye. Pretty soon that baby is at day care all day, and you're rationalizing, "Well, she's with Grandma." Errands and unexpected delays occur, and before you know it, someone—guess who?—has to make dinner! When the last pot is scrubbed, you're so tired you can't wait to put that baby to bed! Your baby's freshest and best hours of the day are spent with someone else.

My heart aches for these little people who are pulled from their warm snuggly beds each morning before daybreak to be thrust into the arms of strangers at kiddie farms across this nation. What will become of them? What will be the fruit of these whose daylight hours have been spent in institutions since birth? What level of comfort will they, in turn, be prepared to give to their own flesh and blood?

No More "Martyr Mom"

Moses' mother didn't have a lot of material goods. She lived in humble circumstances with her husband, son Aaron, daughter Miriam, and new baby son. What she seemed to lack in the natural certainly didn't keep her from living a victorious life. I've lived in plenty, and I've lived in want, and I prefer plenty! But I've had to learn to adapt with joy to whatever circumstances in which I've found myself. I've lived with five kids in a two-bedroom rental house with ugly couches that others loaned to us. I've used a Rubbermaid trunk for a dresser. I've felt humiliated. My paid-off 1995 Toyota is not a beauty! I was laughing the other day, thinking, "I'm in my forties; haven't I earned the privilege of power locks?"

We must learn to be content in our current circumstances if we want God to be able to use us. When we watch too much television and read too many ladies' magazines, we can become grumbly and discontent, feeling underprivileged and wanting. Comparing ourselves to the images paraded on big screens and magazine covers, we can begin to feel like nothing in the eyes of the establishment and, in

> **You know the whispers of the enemy, "Oh, she's a housewife. Ho-hum."**

turn, long to be legitimized by worldly authorities. You know the whispers of the enemy, "Oh, she's a housewife. Ho-hum." On a bad day, you're just an old, tired, out-of-style bag who's busy with the kids. We must resist these vain imaginations and condemning lies so we may, instead, embrace contentment.

Philippians 4:11–13 exhorts us, *I am not saying this because I am in need, for I have learned to be content whatever the circumstances. I know what it is to be in need, and I know what it is to have plenty. I have learned the secret of being content in any and every situation, whether well fed or hungry, whether living in plenty or in want. I can do everything through him who gives me strength.* We don't resign ourselves to staying where we are, yet we make peace with the imperfections of our current, natural circumstances which we're unable to change. At the same time, we're pressing on to take hold of the increase God wants to give us.

You may feel as though you have *so* many limitations. Your list of perceived needs may be overwhelming to your own heart. But with Jesus Christ, you are never at a deficit. Acts 10:34 says that God doesn't play favorites: *Then Peter opened his mouth, and said, "Of a truth I perceive that God is no respecter of persons"* (KJV). But there are conditions. You must choose to meditate on and live in the Word of God. Only by following a righteous lifestyle with strong spirituality will change come. God will give you the victories you are crying out for!

But thanks be to God, who always leads us in triumphal procession in Christ . . . (2 Corinthians 2:14). If I persevere and live by His Word, God *always*—not occasionally, or if I'm lucky, rich, beautiful, married to a perfect man, or have gifted children—but always—leads me into victory in Him. There are no more excuses to live in defeat today!

Happy Mommy

He settles the barren woman in her home as a happy mother of children. Praise the Lord (Psalms 113:9). As you whole-heartedly engage in the huge call to train the children God has given you, you will begin to enjoy your kids in an entirely new way because they will become delightful boys and girls!

Take pleasure in your children, even when they're acting very ordinary. Choose to live with a smile on your face. Leave your children with memories of a mommy who was full of God's patient love and warm touch. If we are grumpy mothers, we leave a stain upon our sons and daughters. Recognize moodiness and depression as predators who will rob your home of God-life! Get up early, begin on your knees, and "purchase" portions from heaven for your family. Proverbs 31:15 says, *She gets up while it is still dark; she provides food for her family* . . . I choose to believe this verse isn't speaking only of eggs and toast, but, more importantly, of the presence of the Holy Spirit and the Bread of Life that truly sustains us. Mom, get the well of your spirit filled up so it spills out onto your children and fills

Take pleasure in your children, even when they're acting very ordinary.

your household with joy! You cannot "make peace" with a dark cloud hanging over your home day after day. Make war against this gloomy weather, and fight for all the promises of God!

CHAPTER SIX

Seize the Day!

We have also come to this hallowed spot to remind America of the fierce urgency of now. This is no time to engage in the luxury of cooling off or to take the tranquilizing drug of gradualism.
—Martin Luther King, Jr.

One day soon, we'll look back and wonder, "What did I do with the last decade?" Amy Grant's 1996 hit sums it up well, "Oh, how the years go by." With either joy or regret you'll reflect upon the days spent, the direction traveled, the choices made, and the accomplishments achieved. The progressive changes seen in the photos of your children will tell the story of how time marched on, while you were perhaps saving, selling, and spending? Wishing, waiting, and wanting? Will you have spent vast amounts of time entertaining yourself? Were you busy regretting days gone by and wrong decisions made? Did you spend enormous emotional energy hugging a grudge or wringing your hands? Were you building your wardrobe and perfecting your body? What will you say? "Wow, I moved four times and made lots of money over the course of time." Or, "I was busy working just making ends meet." Maybe, "Life just took over!" Or perhaps it was all a blur, so you'll admit, "I can't remember!"

And what about the next generation? What were your kids doing with their lives? What seeds did they sow? What focus did they have? What were your goals for them, and were they achieved? What did they eat, watch, and play? What company did they keep? What and who did they pursue? What foundations were laid in their lives? Who were they busy idolizing and emulating? Days, months, and years to spend any way you choose. Are you happy with the course you're setting for them? What fruit will come from the investments you and they are making toward their tomorrows?

How deceptive time is. Before we awake from the chaotic stupor of our fast-paced, twenty-first century lifestyle, sons and daughters will have passed through and closed youth's door, never to open again the innocent days of malleability. Once too busy to pick up that begging youngster, we'd give our left arm to pull Precious right out of that photo album or video and onto our laps so we could drink in his glorious youth, tender grin, longing eyes, and chubby hands. We'd take time for very long hugs and endless, detailed stories of all his day's adventures. We would even ask for more. But right now, we want to pay the bills.

Resolve to live like you won't see this day again, because you won't. Someday you're going to wish you could push that darlin' in his swing or dig in the sand with that little one, but you just never had time for it. You're going to wish you could read David and Goliath 50 times more to that hungry little heart, but guess what? Time's up—door's closed. That's why we must live by faith right where life has us living today! Time doesn't wait. It runs ahead, a harsh taskmaster indeed. No one has lassoed time. It is like the wind; it slips through our busy fingers.

> **Time doesn't wait. It runs ahead, a harsh taskmaster indeed.**

Only God can make time stand still for those of us anxious to please Him. He makes the moments count and reminds us to "STOP!" God gives us opportunity to train and love our children appropriately—not perfectly—in balance with all the other "important" stuff pleading for our attention.

Desperate Measures Must Begin at Birth!

Parents often appear to think there's a switch they'll flip at some point in time and little Susie's going to "come of age." Suddenly around sixteen or seventeen, they can't seem to find the switch on Susie's head. They're watching the chickens come home to roost from all those growing-up years when she was home alone, out late, over-allowanced, and under-prepared for the adult phase she's entering.

Since they didn't parent her at the appropriate time, now Mom and Dad will be parenting her for a very long time, along with the grandbabies who could come on the scene any day now as a result of the lifestyle she's embracing. All those innocent little boyfriends playing kissy-face with her in the rec-room have grown facial hair and now tower over that little girl. But now there isn't much that Mom and Dad can say or do since their window of opportunity to guide her has all but closed with regard to these all-important matters.

Let's make decisions today that we know we can live with tomorrow. Noah built the ark long before the rain began to fall. Let's build now for the tomorrows of our children. Let's diligently prepare the "vehicle" that will safely transport our sons and daughters into their destinies. What a tragedy when a child turns sixteen or seventeen and suddenly Mom and Dad can see the wheels coming off their world. You've seen the telltale signs of trouble ahead: kids with disgruntled and punkish demeanors, "attitude" exuding from every pore. They act exhausted when parents ask for help, are preoccupied with peers, and have no spare time to spend with adults.

Overnight, previously passive parents spring into action. Panic sets in and mothers and fathers will do anything to buy back time and change their kid's course. I've seen many parents take time off work, fly across continents, and spend tens of thousands of dollars to rescue a wayward son or daughter. But during their children's growing-up years it seemed they had no time to consider the outcome of their child's life. This is a sad state of affairs.

We can become distracted from effective parenting as Luke 8:14 details: *But as they go on their way they are choked by life's worries, riches and pleasures, and they do not mature.* The "worries of life" rob our kids' destinies because we set our minds on earthly things and become consumed with the temporal issues at hand. We put off the inevitable and most important issues of life: our sons' and daughters' futures. Then, fifteen years later when we're awakened from our stupor by the condition of our youngsters, we are painfully jarred by the fruit of the life we've been living. We spin our wheels wildly, trying to make up for lost time. But time doesn't wait; it marches on without missing a beat—however cruel it may seem.

Nineteen years ago, at the birth of my second son, I discovered the following lengthy quotation in a gift book, *Children Won't Wait*, by Helen Young. I still can't get through the book without tears of sweet remembrance. I hope it inspires you, too:

> There is a time to treasure every fleeting minute of
> their childhood. Just eighteen precious years to inspire and
> train them. We will not exchange this birthright for a mess of
> pottage called social position, or business success or professional
> reputation. An hour of concern today may save years of heartache
> tomorrow, *the house will wait, the dishes will wait, the new room
> can wait, but children don't wait.* There will be a time when
> there will be no slamming of doors, no toys on the stairs,
> no childhood quarrels, no fingerprints on the wallpaper.
> Then may we look back with joy and not regret. God give
> us wisdom to see that *today* is the day with our children.

That there is no unimportant moment in their lives.
May we know that no other career is so precious,
no other work so rewarding, no other task so urgent.
May we not defer it nor neglect it, but by Thy Spirit accept
it gladly, joyously, and by Thy grace realize that the
time is short and our time is now, for *children won't wait!*[4]

Kids Take Time

There are no shortcuts to good parenting. By interviewing those who seem to have muddled through the maze of parenting and found success, you may save yourself some blunders. But good parenting, successful training of world-changers, can only be accomplished by spending *large quantities of time.*

We don't argue that growing a garden takes time, gaining a college degree takes time, waiting for a newborn to arrive still takes right around nine months, and building a house out of sticks and bricks takes the better part of a year, no matter what the contractor may promise you! Then why do we think we can churn out a human being of substance, depth, and character in a mere fraction of the time we spend at the office each day? What makes us expect that by dropping our children off at youth group to hang with their peers at a church building, water park, or activity center, they'll come home filled with vision, promise, and empowered for God's kingdom?

Do we really believe in our heart of hearts that after investing such small increments of time, our return will be large? I don't think so. We may comfort ourselves temporarily with the popular notion that *quality,* rather than *quantity,* time benefits our children, but what we're seeing in our kids *with our own eyes* is telling us a much different story. It is the rare child indeed who will thrive with very little input from their parents' hands and hearts on a daily basis. Yes, developing great kids is costly in every way. Just as in any profit-making scheme, the shares you purchase in this parenting investment package are expensive, especially for the first eighteen years or so. But with time, the dividends will bring an extremely valuable return.

> **It is the rare child indeed who will thrive with very little input from their parents' hands and hearts on a daily basis.**

---

[4] © Young, Helen M. *Children Won't Wait* (Texas: Brownlow Publishing Company, Inc. 1985).

Tender Saplings

In many yards you'll see a young tree with a metal pole on each side of its thin trunk. From each pole extends a thick band looped around the trunk, pulled taut in both directions. The purpose of these bands is to force the trunk to maintain an erect posture and impose undeviating growth on the immature tree. To me, it is a picture of parenting in the early years.

How cruel to allow a sapling to grow its own way, becoming all gnarly and mutated, never to achieve its intended height and health and fruitfulness. We must work while there is time and the conditions are most favorable! A sapling bends easily, but if we wait even five years, it takes amputation to bring about any substantial change. Psalms 90:12 offers a relevant prayer: *Teach us to number our days aright, that we may gain a heart of wisdom.* Let's remember that every day counts.

Don't ignore the unrest in your heart and rationalize it away as obsessive or unnatural control. It's very likely the voice of God urging you to take the time necessary to establish firm boundaries around your kids, so you will have a healthy garden, producing sweet fruit!

> **Don't ignore the unrest in your heart and rationalize it away as obsessive or unnatural control. It's very likely the voice of God . . .**

Someday

What is your opus? What is your masterpiece, your life's work, the culmination of your years of labor and perseverance? What will you have to show for your number of days spent upon the earth? Will it be a grand estate stretched across acres of rolling hills, hugging the ocean? Or perhaps a massive, diversified retirement account that E. F. Hutton would admire. Maybe you're working on a network marketing scheme that is sure to line your pockets for years to come.

Many parents are busy putting off living life in the now while embracing the lie of "someday." Luxurious retirement is their vision. They labor diligently, placing their hard-earned dollars in investments to grow, accrue interest, and appreciate considerably for enjoyment . . . someday. It's always good to save and plan, but an obsession with worldly investments can consume so much of life. What a waste this has proved to be for so many human beings!

This promise of ecstasy, security, and indulgence may be realized to some degree, but it unfairly consumes countless hours of life *now*. While ignoring their children, many invest huge portions of thought and energy into "someday," working overtime hours, accumulating wages, and delaying pleasure for a tomorrow that may never take place.

Those who do realize their financial goals are often left eating banquets alone. Once too busy to have invested considerable time in their children and grandchildren, they now find themselves devoid of rich human relationships. Others are confronted by disease, accident, old age, or other unplanned circumstances which rob their latter years of the "ultimate goal."

Let's spend a good portion of our resources *now* by investing in our relationships. We cannot take our perfect lawn, our luxury sedan, our football team, our golf swing, or our fit bodies into eternity with us. Only our relationships with others are lasting. A childhood poem comes to mind:

> *Just one life,*
> *'Twill soon be past.*
> *Only what's done,*
> *In Christ will last.*

Let us redeem the time even today! Let us highly resolve to live life on purpose with our sons and daughters.

In a day and age when the masses are foolishly squandering this valuable resource of time, Ephesians 5:15–17 clearly exhorts us *to be very careful, then, how you live—not as unwise but as wise, making the most of every opportunity, because the days are evil. Therefore do not be foolish, but understand what the Lord's will is.* Let us be done with lesser things and wisely employ this fleeting asset called time!

Refuse to imbibe the tranquilizing drug of gradualism. This very moment, make a list of those things the Holy Spirit is speaking to you about and put it on your mirror, in your Bible, next to your bed—where it will be a constant reminder of where you and your family are headed. Focus on and begin, with God's help, to change one thing at a time. Take hope in Philippians 1:6, *Being confident of this, that he who began a good work in you will carry it on to completion until the day of Christ Jesus.* Seize today! Put yesterday behind you, and run toward the vision He is setting before you!

> **Let us redeem the time even today! Let us highly resolve to live life on purpose with our sons and daughters.**

CHAPTER SEVEN

No Ordinary Child Will Do!

Don't let anyone look down on you because you are young, but set an example for the believers in speech, in life, in love, in faith, and in purity.

—1 Timothy 4:12

A t conception, Moses had within his nature the mantle of a deliverer. Woven into his being was a call to national leadership. We must seek God to tap into and develop the giftings and mantles with which our kids are created. According to God's Word, our job description is waiting for us at birth! Ephesians 2:10 clearly states: *We are God's workmanship, created in Christ Jesus to do good works, **which God prepared in advance for us to do***. Also Jeremiah 1:5 reminds us of the principle that our destiny is written even before we arrive. *"Before I formed you in the womb I knew you, before you were born I set you apart; **I appointed you as a prophet to the nations."***

I have a burning desire to see parents grasp the possibility that lies within their little ones. As they do, the ramifications will prove to be life-changing for them and their children. This revelation of who their children are meant to become will fuel these parents' engines, thus moving them to action! This action will propel their kids forward into their destinies, thereby nullifying the devil's schemes for them and those whose lives they'll impact.

The world is waiting for our children's greatness. Why are we winking at mediocrity? Why are we blessing and encouraging normalcy? Our kids should reflect God's glory in this dark and perverse generation and be above reproach. We've got to aim for building *extraordinary* children: not according to the usual custom or regular plan, but far beyond the ordinary degree, measure, and limit. They should be unusual, exceptional, and just plain remarkable.

> **The world is waiting for our children's greatness. Why are we winking at mediocrity?**

On the contrary, *ordinary* is defined as: a common occurrence, quality, or ability. It was apparent to me at the births of my five sons that each was *no . . . ordinary . . . child.* Time stood still in our vast universe as I drank in the beauty of each of these tiny miracles. This was not another mouth to feed or a profitable tax deduction. These custom-designed creations were brimming with life, arriving at the appointed moment and poised to impact history's timeline. Each shouted his gigantic potential to the world around him! No words could describe the holy hush hanging thickly in the air all around.

You, too? Of course! For never has there been even one ordinary child born into this world. No matter what his physical condition or worldly worth, I am convinced that an inherent greatness resides within every fiber of his being. Planted in his DNA are the seeds of a deliverer. His substance awaits us, his parents, to spring into action with all the resources available to us to use in seeing this potential realized.

Why am I so confident of your child's huge potential? Because he or she is a child of the King! We all take after our dads in some form or fashion. The Word of God tells us that, *We are His offspring* (Acts 17:28). And consider Genesis 1:26 where God said, *Let us make man in our image, in our likeness.* Whether newborn, toddler, teen, adult, or elderly, we are clearly God's posterity.

How can we agree with the Word by claiming the living God as our ancestor, but not possess His distinct characteristics or, at the very least, shadows of His attributes? Ponder for a moment the intricate, complex, multi-faceted, and brilliant composition of any human being on the planet. Even sin-sick human beings, marred by the effects of an ungodly, destructive lifestyle, still bear the likeness of their heavenly Father in some apparent way.

> **Let's not judge our children according to their history, but according to their destiny!**

Ask God to allow you to see your child through His perfect, discerning, and gracious eyes. Let's not judge our children according to their history, but according to their destiny! Let's not say such high ideals are impossible, for *with God all things are possible!* (Matthew 19:26). Let's stop feeding on common magazines and employing common child-raising techniques, so we can stop producing common children who don't have an edge.

My heart is beating passionately for this: We can raise a generation of Moses-types. How do we begin? First, we must always keep our vision before us, ahead of the dirty diapers, the ever-dwindling groceries, a faraway Grandma who cannot help, relentless bills, and all the daily realities that want to distract us. We must raise our vision higher. I'll tell you what my vision is: I want to raise sons who are godly leaders in the earth and who become men who make an impact. I see human tanks rolling across the nations as God's weapons of mass destruction, which He uses to raze the kingdom of hell. I want you to raise sons and daughters who are just the same.

I'm sobered and grieved in my heart over the condition of children in America and in other parts of the world. I bear this grief in my heart night and day. I can't walk past strangers pushing strollers without becoming stirred as I ponder the life that sits in that baby carriage. I'm moved as I consider the absolute dynamite awaiting detonation in that little person. I see the world-changer who lives inside every frame. I want this vision to beat in your heart, too. I long for us to pray fervently, even with pain, for our children because we realize our mechanical religious gestures will not ignite their explosive potential. If our prayer is a blasé: "Oh God, bless the kids," then we might as well cross our fingers or buy a lucky charm.

Our Kids Should Be Stars

I was reading an article on Arnold and Maria (Shriver) Schwarzenegger's family life from the *Sacramento Bee* newspaper. Most people know Arnold as a leading actor and politician in the state of California and wife Maria as a television journalist. Here are some highlights from the article, published when Arnold became Governor of California:

> "Maria and Arnold made a decision very early to preserve the privacy of their children," said Roberta Hollander, a producer in the Los Angeles bureau of CBS News and a close friend of the couple for the past two decades. "Maria's major focus as these days unfold will be to make sure her children continue to have normal lives."
>
> Although they have a substantial staff of household helpers, Schwarzenegger and Shriver do the parenting, friends said.
>
> "They are openly loving and affectionate toward their children but also are strong disciplinarians who constantly stress the importance of hard work and helping others," said Wanda McDaniel Ruddy, a public relations executive for Giorgio Armani in Los Angeles and one of Shriver's closest friends.
>
> "The older children do chores, including laundry, cleaning their rooms and clearing their plates from the table, and all of them write their own thank you notes, acknowledging gifts," said Ruddy. "These children are incredibly respectful, incredibly well-mannered,"

she said. "They're not robotic at all, but when you walk into a room they make eye contact and greet guests by name. They have impeccable manners."

Hollander agreed, "I have seen them at parties, with tons of kids, and you would never, ever know they were the children of stars," she said. "It's impossible to tell who are the stars' kids, who are the housekeeper's kids, who are the rich kids and who are the poor kids. They're just fun, happy, normal kids."

"They can't slack off in school, they can't slack off in their homework," she said. "Arnold had a very strong disciplinary background, and he is passing that on to his children. He wants them to know that you can't take anything for granted in this world. You have to work for things."

No television is allowed in [their] household on weeknights, but—except for Sunday church services—weekends are reserved for fun, jam-packed with recreational activities from softball games to soccer matches, dance recitals, basketball practices and sleepovers, friends said.

All in all, Hollander said, the Schwarzenegger family is "surprisingly normal," and determined to stay that way. "I have watched Maria and Arnold grow their children for almost 14 years now, and it has been a real eye-opener . . . a lesson for us all in everything that a loving family should be. That's not going to change."[5]

This man and woman appear to be raising excellent children. They are not claiming to be powering kingdom-builders, just everyday people. They could have lots of reasons for being too busy for hands-on parenting, but instead they have made it a priority to train their children well. They are succeeding in this task because God's principles work! *What are we doing with the kids God has given us?*

Do you know what I find disturbing? This Schwarzenegger story should not be unusual stuff. This should be absolutely normal for those of us who live for Jesus. Unfortunately in my experience, church kids can be some of the worst kids to be around. Unmannerly, overly indulged brats are running through the halls of church buildings with reckless abandon, while parents stand by doing nothing. It's time to raise our vision.

Glory of God

It should be normal to meet believers' children and see the glory of God resting on them. What do I mean by that? I think it's really quite simple. Let's not over-spiritualize this stuff and miss the mark. What are some earmarks of a child who carries God's glory?

---

[5] © The Sacramento Bee, 2003.

- quick obedience when Mom or Dad gives a command
- displaying a right spirit in our homes and at the grocery store, even when things don't go Junior's way
- no prejudice or cynicism toward others, even if they're an ignoramus
- holding material things very loosely
- being generous at all times—even toward their siblings—with what God has graciously given them
- a self-sacrificing attitude—readiness to serve others at one's personal expense
- humility when they win the game
- kindness—even when others don't deserve it
- expressing sincere gratitude for every little blessing
- a patient and self-controlled manner with younger siblings
- a happy heart for others who get something Susie wanted to have
- withholding hateful words when they want to spew
- a tender heart toward the weak and poor

It's not the time to create kids who will simply fill a cog in our world's system. It's time to raise up a new breed of young people who will surpass the status quo! Let's aim to build children with magnanimous character. If people aren't noticing something special in our kids and commenting on it regularly, I believe we're missing it. We better take stock and if necessary, bring change to our households.

> **It's time to raise up a new breed of young people who will surpass the status quo!**

CHAPTER EIGHT

Sons and Daughters

Children are our most valuable natural resource.
—Herbert Hoover

Praise the LORD. Blessed is the man who fears the LORD, who finds great delight in his commands. **His children will be mighty in the land;** *the generation of the upright will be blessed.*
—Psalms 112:1–2

D are to believe God that, in the midst of a wicked and perverse generation, we can have sons and daughters who are Daniels. I believe we should raise our kids to be the cream of the crop—excellent in every way: diet, exercise, attitude, education, and understanding. They should stand out, head and shoulders above their peers. When King Nebuchadnezzar besieged Jerusalem, he asked to see the finest stock of young men that Israel had to offer.

Daniel 1:3 tells us, *Then the king ordered Ashpenaz, chief of his court officials, to bring in some of the Israelites from the royal family and the nobility.* He was particularly impressed with four Israelite young men who consequently were used in an amazing way to turn the nation around. The king didn't ask these pious youths to recite the law and the prophets. Actually, he liked how they looked! "How unspiritual," you might say. But like it or not, it's fact. These were not effeminate, frail, pale-skinned, or cookie-cutter, religious boys. These were robust young men.

The king was impressed with their knowledge of literature and current events and their fit bodies. In the words of my son Gabriel, "They were ripped!" They exuded vigorous energy in body and mind. I imagine that their skin was clear, and they had glowing countenances. Their excellent attitudes and gentlemanly behavior held the king captive. These were unequalled and bold four-star young men who could carry on an intelligent conversation concerning government, politics, and history. This golden character wasn't mined by sitting in front of the television or playing computer games all day. Uh-uh.

> **This golden character wasn't mined by sitting in front of the television or playing computer games all day. Uh-uh.**

Boys or Sort-of Boys?

There's never been a better time than now for Dr. James Dobson to release his latest best-seller, *Bringing Up Boys*. The best part about the book is that it presents a convincing and very necessary argument that (*surprise!*) boys are much different than girls. Home schooling pioneer Gregg Harris said it so well: "Most moms want their boys to grow up to be good little girls." It would be very funny if it weren't so true!

I'm seeing this problem firsthand in my own neighborhood. Samuel cannot come over to our house because he always gets dirty (ee gads, the sky is falling!), and the boys get so *aggressive* playing "army." His Mom would rail on him about his appearance every time he left our home. He's pale, skinny, and he talks like a girl. His shorts are too short, and he pulls them up to his chin. Poor kid. He could have been a boy! A household like ours with five boys and an arsenal of harmless plastic weapons obviously cannot be trusted in our politically-correct world. He's mysteriously never been back, though he was happy as a weasel in a hen house when he played in our yard.

D-I-R-T seems to be a four-letter word to so many preppie moms nowadays. Why, Junior's little GAP trousers might be spoilt! Better to spoil the labels than spoil the masculine side of our sons, don'tcha' think? Surely you've noticed how many pretty boys are waiting on you in restaurants, clothing shops, and hotels. It's so fashionable and acceptable in our culture to be feminized if you're a male. Who's raising these kids? Is it Hollywood's homosexuals? Where was Dad when little Junior began his effeminate gestures? Was he busy playing virtual NASCAR on his computer? Watching television? Networking?

I grieve for young lives squandered by lethargic and preoccupied parents. I look at so many boys around us: either gussied up and womanish or with pants sagging down their rears, they're wasted blobs of nothingness, not a clue where they're going. If we're too busy to raise real men, then face it guys, we're just too busy!

What Kind of Daughters Are We Raising?

In our gushing pride over their God-given abilities and beauty, we parents can lose our heads when it comes to raising our daughters. We are so busy coddling and indulging them that we are creating beauty queens and princesses, instead of what God desires. God can't do much with a high-maintenance girl. You can spot her a mile away. She knows how to tan, pedicure, and spa, but doesn't have a clue about how to cook, work, build, or persevere. If you stand her up and draw a circle around her, there's her big wide world. "It's all about me," sums up her condition.

> Let's be careful not to overly emphasize this world's system, parroting Egypt's values to the detriment of our daughters' God-given callings.

Let's be careful not to overly emphasize this world's system, parroting Egypt's values to the detriment of our daughters' God-given callings. Let's not direct daughters solely toward careers that prepare them for large bank accounts without considering their mother-hearts. Yes, some of our young ladies of today are destined to become professional women of tomorrow, employed in lucrative positions of great influence in our communities. But far more will be needed to train up the next generation. Queens and princesses don't make great mothers most of the time; they're so full of their own cares. Our young ladies will have to have a servant's heart to flourish in this calling of motherhood.

God is looking for a workhorse; these are women who don't collapse under heavy burdens. These young ladies have an eye to see a need and a servant's heart to meet that need. Our local church is packed full of such kingdom young women. They aren't dull, dowdy, and bored with nothing better to do than show up at church functions. These are vivacious, well-groomed, and attractive young ladies who can always be found caring for the babies, serving in the children's ministry, making meals for the sick, serving the single parents, making disciples of younger believers, opening their homes for hospitality, reaching out to the lost, cleaning and decorating the church building for special functions, praying for the hurting, ad infinitum.

These young women realize they have been chosen by God for "such a time as this," and they are spending their lives on Jesus and His purposes in the earth. These are quality young gals who have allowed the Lord to develop them into ruthless, fierce, unbending, courageous, militant women, with backbones of steel and foreheads of flint. They are modeling to the world around them what a real young lady should be all about.

Modest Dress

While I'm on the subject of training our daughters, let's talk about fashion. All girls love to be trendy, and they can be especially so these days if they happen to get their fair share of good genes, producing buxom tops and curvaceous bottoms. It seems to me that the designers are pin-pointing a female's hottest spots with their latest offerings. Add to these fashions an indiscreet public presentation and a loud and flirtatious manner while mixing socially with young men, and we've got disaster waiting at the door!

The majority of media sources in our modern cultures are leading the way by promoting such lack of discretion. It runs the gamut from clothing, perfume, and make-up ads to teen magazines, lewd music videos, soft-drink commercials, and compact disc covers—not to mention lyrics! Our daughters are relentlessly inundated with these illicit romantic and sexually suggestive images! What a powerful weapon against our children! We can see the grievous fruit born of these sinister seeds in the lives of so many dear, misguided young girls today.

> **Beware of what you're encouraging your daughters to enjoy.**

We must be diligent dads and moms who will better direct our daughters into less trivial pursuits than emulating the latest silicone boob that be-bops across the video screen. Many of our modern-day teen idols come across more like pubescent strumpets than musical artists. Beware of what you're encouraging your daughters to enjoy.

Unfortunately, I'm seeing a lot of young ladies, thirteen going on twenty-five, dressed like hookers. Even worse, Christian parents are putting their stamp of approval on these promiscuous-looking, eyeball-popping creations by forking over the dough to pay for them, enjoying their daughter's attractive display like mindless adolescents themselves, or, at the very least, allowing them out of the house in these shameful get-ups! What are we thinking?

Men are wired by God to experience delight and energy upon viewing what God has created in the female body. However, these pleasurable views were meant for the privacy of marriage. Stirring up a guy's impulses to the point of causing him to stumble morally is a real issue. 1 Corinthians 10:32 and Romans 14:21 address the matter, and we shouldn't lightly dismiss their teaching. What man, young or old, can worship God freely when parading in front of his all-too-human eyeballs is a sight beyond description, begging for his attention?

I cannot espouse that this is exclusively the "man's problem." I've heard this trite statement thrown out from time to time by women. No, this conflict has two components, and one is the primary antagonist in my opinion. Chickies, we better beware of what we're wearing and what we're allowing our girls to wear. Our beauty, and our daughter's beauty, must *originate from* our inner being.

True Beauty

1 Peter 3:3–4 says, *Your beauty should not come from outward adornment, such as braided hair and the wearing of gold jewelry and fine clothes. Instead, it should be that of your inner self, the unfading beauty of a gentle and quiet spirit, which is of great worth in God's sight.* That rare, superior substance within cannot be found in a bottle (darn!), manufactured, borrowed, or purchased with money. Without this inner quality, all the other exterior stuff won't take us very far. No amount of make-up, perfume, physical exercise, or education can hide an ugly spirit.

I'm not against working to be physically fit and attractive. I want to be the absolute best I can be in every way. If I let myself go and become obese, unkempt, and matronly, I'm not godlier for it, and my husband would certainly not be more blessed. It's hypocritical to have led a husband to believe he'd found his "babe" when we were dating, only to later become a slob, weighing 100 pounds more with stringy hair and acne. I want to be Gregory's earth angel well into my nineties! I want to stir his passions and consume all his romantic thoughts, and that takes diligence and self-control. But even with a trim figure and trendy style, without the real goods of a pure spirit and a holy heart, I'm simply not going to be desirable.

The masses of supermodel wannabes across the globe don't have access to this fountain of youth flowing from 1 Peter three. How fortunate and to be envied we godly women are to be privy to such beauty secrets, and what a legacy to hand down to our daughters. Even in matters of health and beauty, counter-culture is where we've got to live!

Plants and Pillars

Deliver me and rescue me from the hands of foreigners whose mouths are full of lies, whose right hands are deceitful. Then our sons in their youth will be like well-nurtured plants, and our daughters will be like pillars carved to adorn a palace, says Psalms 144:11–12. In our nation today, the lying and deceitful hearts of men who are foreign to God's ways and purposes are prescribing a strategy for our children's lives. It is a strategy that will take them where we do not want them to go.

If we continue to do what we've always done with regard to training our sons and daughters, but expect a different result in them, we are insane. Let's do something we've never done, to get something both we and our children have never had before! Boldly ask God to help you build children who are indeed the plants and pillars you long to

> **Let's do something we've never done, to get something both we and our children have never had before!**

raise! They will smell different, look different, and act different. Let's believe God for His glory to rest upon our children. These are the dreams I hold dear. Oh parents, hear the cry of God's heart for your sons and daughters!

CHAPTER NINE

Without a Vision, the Parents Dwell Carelessly

Then the LORD answered me and said: **Write the vision,** *and make it plain on tablets, that he may run who reads it. For the vision is yet for an appointed time; but* **at the end it will speak, and it will not lie. Though it tarries, wait for it; because it will surely come, it will not tarry.**

—Habakkuk 2:2–3 NKJV

O ur *vision* must be the *destiny* God has hidden for our sons and daughters. Our mission is to uncover this divine purpose. How hard we work to provide our kids with everything we think they need to become what others expect them to be! But is this the proper *vision* for them? How feverishly we labor to attain a standard considered acceptable by society, yet will this lead to our children's *appointed destiny*?

Do you have a vision for your kids? Would you be able to write it out quickly at this very moment? If so, what's your plan for achieving your vision? *A vision without a plan is called a fantasy.* To enable our sons and daughters to reach the destination of leadership, we must have a clear road map to get them there! Lots of disappointed parents can tell you that a hazy approach to guiding children in life does not get them where they need to go.

I Have a Dream

I dream of integrity in the character of my five sons. Not wealth. Not fame. Not talent screaming from every pore of their bodies, but a good name. Proverbs 22:1 says, *A good name is more desirable than great riches; to be esteemed is better than silver or gold.*

Folks should be clamoring to hire our sons and daughters! When circumstances shift and our children give notice to their employers, they should leave some very big shoes to fill. I believe corporate executives will stand in line to find a good man, one who keeps his word and gives a full day's work for a full day's wage. I feel assured that if my sons have character, they can write their own ticket in this world.

1 Timothy 4:8 reminds us, *Godliness has value for all things, holding promise for both the present life and the life to come.* Godliness describes God-like character and is the key to success in life for our sons and daughters! Our world doesn't need more slick dudes. We need unusual men and women filled with godly wisdom, who stand head and shoulders above their shallow, partying peers.

I don't want "quality kids," according to this world's system. I want kids who set the measure. Stop pursuing the wrong path for your kids with the false promise of worldly success! The same profane voices which express contempt for our Judeo-Christian ethics, ridicule our religious persuasion, and bash our extravagant worship and militant commitment to God's Word, will also beg for the privilege of hiring our unusual children to further their financial endeavors.

Drowning in the Dailies

Parents without a vision dwell carelessly. As the scent of baby lotion fades, the "dailies" can set in to bog us down and blur our vision. You know well the tedium of everyday life. It's all that stuff that has to be done: toddlers to chase, meals to make, bills to juggle, friends to call, carpets to vacuum, tile to mop, diapers to change, dogs to walk, dentists to see, taxes to pay, new shoes to buy, baby-sitters to schedule, weddings to rejoice over, and funerals to cry at . . . it never ends.

> **Sunrise, sunset, and little by little, too many of us parents forget the divine promise residing within our offspring.**

Sunrise, sunset, and little by little, too many of us parents forget the divine promise residing within our offspring. Blinded to the higher purpose of unlocking the leadership potential in our own flesh and blood, we live predictable lives, blending into the culture around us, playing by the rules, and compromising our standards while lowering our expectations.

We begin to live in the slums of just being a housewife or a bread-winner, when we could be polishing, straightening, and sharpening arrows that will penetrate the darkness and bring in the nations. What are we producing for tomorrow's church leadership? What are we producing that is going to change our world? It is high time we realize our destinies lie in our dailies.

I saw a young father with his first child. Ever so carefully and uncertainly he cradled his new son in his loving arms. Awkwardly trying to hold but not crush, protect but not bruise, he and his wife appeared tentative and overly concerned about this new little bundle. Oh, how the days go by. These, who we once so delicately and passionately cared for, receive decreasing levels of parental care and concern. We can become overly confident, a bit cocky, and even presumptuous in our parenting.

It would do us well to maintain our careful posture of deep concern and humility, preserving the fresh "awe" over the privilege of handling a newborn little miracle. Let us echo the heart cry of Samson's dad in Judges 13:12: *What is to be the rule for this young man?* In other words, "How do we bring up our son? I am only a little child myself; how do I do this?"

Correctly Assessing Our Kids

A proper assessment assures us we're on the right track, heading toward the vision God has given us for our children. I have to ask, how are we assessing our kids? Most schools administer broad assessment tests once toward the end of the year, while report cards go out quarterly. I don't put a lot of stock in what the S.A.T., C.A.T or the I.T.B.S say about my kids. They've always tested well on these, but the scores don't carry a lot of weight with me. In our home, their progress is monitored daily and their character assessed relentlessly; these are the tests I'm concerned about. I don't care if they've read every book that Nietzsche or Darwin has written and memorized it backwards. It doesn't matter if they've been invited to honors classes. At the end of the day, it's meaningless if there's not character, integrity, godliness, and world-changing, eternal purpose in their lives.

> When assessing our children, we must continually resist worldly wisdom that is diametrically opposed to what God wants to do in our parenting.

1 Corinthians 2:6–7 teaches us that human wisdom will almost always *war against* the wisdom which God brings. The wisdom of the rulers of this age results in nothing. It is a secret wisdom of God that we need and must diligently seek. It is indeed the mind of Christ working through us! When assessing our children, we must continually resist worldly wisdom that is diametrically opposed to what God wants to do in our parenting.

If my children don't possess prized qualities of distinction like perseverance, respect for authority, quick obedience, faithfulness, and a solid work ethic, then what kind of impact can they possibly have in our dark world? If my boys don't hold a correct and righteous worldview, display active compassion to a hurting world, and desire to build

God's kingdom above all else, then in actuality, no matter what the test scores tell me, I would have failed to produce a successful man.

John Taylor Gatto, former public school educator, had this to say about the children he taught for over two decades in the public system:

> The children I teach are indifferent to the adult world. The children I teach have almost no curiosity. The children I teach are cruel to each other; they lack compassion for misfortune; they laugh at weakness; they have contempt for people whose need for help shows too plainly. The children I teach are dependent, passive, and timid in the presence of new challenges.[6]

This assessment is troubling. How many educated children of our day would be similar? That is a specimen you and I don't want to produce. A person who is highly educated, but without character, is an educated idiot. God knows there are more than enough of them populating the earth as it is. Many of them teach at our universities!

Don't hear what I'm not saying. Education is important. In fact, it's so important to me that I've labored long and hard educating my children for the better part of 20 years. I take their life preparation very seriously, but all my eggs aren't in that education basket.

This world's system of assessing our children is based on their good looks, athletic prowess, personal charisma, academic standing, fine arts talent, and so on. This information is collected and used to compare our kids with others their age. Comparisons are odious to God and a death knell to us and our children. And, although a child may excel in any or all of these categories, he may still greatly lack true substance in his life. Sadly enough, grandparents, educators, and adult friends aren't always a good litmus test either. Depending on what their basis for evaluation is, they might be out in left field in their assessment of *your* child.

I hold cautiously any public opinion presented apart from God and the truth of His Word and purpose as these relate to my child. I'm not endorsing lone-ranger parents with an independent spirit, but I am saying the buck stops with you. You have to own the responsibility of hearing God first and foremost for your children. What does God think? How does your child rate in His economy? Are the goals you're striving to achieve lining up with His vision and destiny for your kids?

---

[6] Gatto, John T. Dumbing Us Down (Philadelphia: New Society Publishers, 1992), pp. 30–32.

CHAPTER TEN

Getting God's Strategy for Your Children

It is not necessary to do extraordinary things to get extraordinary results.

—Warren Buffet

Moses' folks were in a tight spot. They needed a strategy! Their dilemma called for stuff that money cannot buy. Is your back against the wall? You may be feeling weak, but God's Word assures us in 2 Peter 1:3 that we already have *everything we need for life and godliness.* We don't live by our feelings, but by the truth of God's Word. Just like pilots who can't trust what they see out the cockpit window and have to fly by instruments, we too often must fly by the instrument of God's Word. When everything swirling around us seems to contradict His truth, here in His Word in black and white, we're told that we *lack nothing* for living in godliness.

I'm not saying it always comes easily. You've got to read the fine print on this one! Look at the next half of the verse. 2 Peter 1:3 emphasizes that provision comes *through our knowledge of him who called us by his own glory and goodness.* It's only through our *knowledge of Him* that we obtain this promise. It's as if we must reach into heaven to grasp those divine resources and pull them down to earth where they're needed! Nothing is automatic in the kingdom except for God's love for us—everything we aspire to requires effort.

For Mom and Dad this translates into: Get on your knees and ask God for a practical strategy to raise Junior. Your little darling is custom-made by God and only He can give you the customized plan for how to train up this human being. Knock, seek, ask, and give God no rest until you hear His voice and get the answers you need! This isn't a one-time deal. Time and again, in what feels like desperation, I've found myself in my secret place with the Most High God, seeking answers to my questions about His strategy for my sons.

> **So much is up to us. God waits for us to move toward Him, so that He can lead us on the perfect path for our children.**

Moses' parents didn't have a lot to work with, but as they followed the stick-and-mud plan God gave them, their son was spared from certain death. The stakes haven't changed. It's life or death for our kids. So much is up to us. God waits for us to move toward Him, so that He can lead us on the perfect path for our children.

We've got to get a strategy from God, just like Moses' parents did. It was not a good time to be expecting a child in Egypt. On the day when her little Moses had at last arrived, Mom could have flipped out. Her reaction could have been up-in-arms anxiety, dust flying, tears flowing, and generally making life miserable for her husband and friends. But we don't see that. We don't see Dad pacing the floor and asking, "Why did You do this to us, God? What were You thinking?"

No, I believe these folks cried out to God in faith. They did not allow doubt to rule them, even when the circumstances looked bad, and the rains came, and the winds blew. No, their faith increased, and when they saw that baby, they said, "This isn't just another newborn. Something unusual is happening here. God, we need a strategy. Oh, we can hide this infant for awhile, but we need a long-term plan."

I don't care how rich you are or how poor you are, there is a strategy from God for you, wherever you are sitting. I've lived out of cardboard boxes in a modest dwelling, and I've lived in what I would consider a palace of a home. God will give us a strategy if all we have is a box to live in. I remember one year: we had no money for books for school, and a large part of the strategy God had given us to safely transport our sons into the future was home schooling. I remember being on the verge of a panic attack because I couldn't buy books and September was approaching. Through a set of circumstances, I felt like God said, "Denise, this is the book you need." The Bible. It seemed too simple.

I could have sat there for days moaning, "Oh God, I'm gonna fail. Poor me, I'm finished," becoming depressed about my lack. Believe me, I was tempted! Thankfully, by God's grace, something rose up in me and I decided, "I'm going to plant my feet here, and I'm going to believe God." Like W.H. Murray's quote affirms, Providence will meet us! Remember, if we'll stand and decide, "Providence moves, too."

We began to open the Word of God in a greater way that year. We kept detailed charts of our sons' progress of reading the Bible through. To celebrate their completion of reading, we had a very special meal and invited significant men of influence in their lives to join us. Everything came together in the end, and those three boys ended up academically prepared, going to college at sixteen (for those of you who worry about the details!). As they say, hindsight is 20/20, but in my moment of great need, I couldn't see the future, and I was on the brink. God came through for us that fall several years ago, and He will do the same for you.

It doesn't matter how big your wallet is. It doesn't matter what your friends think. God will give you a strategy or, put another way, *a practical plan*. It's my firm conviction that every biblical principle demands a very practical response. How can the Bible be relevant to our daily lives, if we're unable to apply it in specific ways? If you have a vision of what you want to see developed in your children, then you must know that without a practical plan, you might simply have a fantasy. I challenge you to regularly write down the specifics of what God is leading you to implement. It might be as simple as sticks and mud, but this is your strategy from heaven.

In my opinion many Christians put too much stock in super-spiritual, subjective experiences, but not enough in the objective truth of God's Word, applied as a daily lifestyle. Dreams, visions, and prophetic words about our children can all be very encouraging, but we have to have a disciplined plan to get them where God wants to take them. As I said already, let me say again with emphasis: *Every biblical principle demands a very practical response.*

Yes, Moses' folks wanted his life to be spared, but they didn't just toss up a prayer and cross their fingers. I believe they prayed unceasingly until they got a *practical plan*. This unprecedented strategy could only have originated in the mind of God. What human being would be so stupid as to think a common basket could save a life? Armed Egyptian soldiers were bearing down on them. We're talking about the Super Power of the world at that time.

But oh, how our sovereign God loves to contradict the wisdom of the wise with His simple strategies! In 1 Corinthians 1:19 we see God's clear intention: *I will destroy the wisdom of the wise; the intelligence of the intelligent I will frustrate.*

I've watched a pencil and a sheet of paper combined with a borrowed library book and a tattered Bible become a powerful recipe for valuable education against the forces of darkness in my sons' lives. What secrets God has for us as parents! What heavenly schemes He longs to share with us if we'll only take the time to listen!

> **What secrets God has for us as parents! What heavenly schemes He longs to share with us if we'll only take the time to listen!**

Perhaps the following concept of a "kingdom filter" will aid you in finding your practical plan. This filter has become an integral part of the strategy God has given to us, as we've endeavored to bring up our young leaders.

Kingdom Filters

There is a kingdom filter we must develop for our households. Our filter is formed by the values we hold dear. This filter is positioned at the gate of our homes and lives, and it stands as a resolute dam against the rushing current of harmful invaders from our society and culture. The password for access is "kingdom purpose," and very few suitors are granted permission to enter. Instead of a list of rules on our walls, we need this kingdom filter over our lives.

Is this filter in place at the door of your home and family? Without it, you'll live in a perpetual state of indecision, confusion, and frustration as all the options of life, many of which should be filtered out, pummel you from every direction. With this filter in place, you'll play an offensive game of purpose in life, rather than a defensive game of red-alert reaction.

Kingdom filters declare that we've said an unequivocal "yes" to God and to building His kingdom. That means our children will give their strength to the kingdom. Period. We won't have to say "no" a lot because the "yes" to God settles a lot of questionable matters in advance. It helps us quickly determine what takes priority in our homes.

After 25 years of serving in leadership in local churches, I've observed many young families' priorities. "Well, we can't come to prayer meeting 'cause we have ballet." "We can't come to cell group 'cause we have soccer every Sunday." "Well, we've got basketball four nights a week." "We've got play group, so I can't come." "I'd love to take her a meal, but I'm hosting a candle party!" None of these extracurricular activities in themselves is bad or sinful, and if we're Spirit-led, they can be avenues of training, preparation, and evangelistic outreach. But in a society like ours, where activities are trying to drive our lives, we have to be sure our lifestyles teach our children that the kingdom of God is truly the priority of our homes.

> . . . in a society like ours, where activities are trying to drive our lives, we have to be sure our lifestyles teach our children that the kingdom of God is truly the priority of our homes.

We're all busy, but we better make sure we're busy about the kingdom. My boys have wanted to play football for fifteen years. I called to check on the possibility and found it demanded participation seven days a week! I said, "Sorry guys; that doesn't fit into our lives. Get a ball, grab your friends, go out in the street, and play football." And you know, I don't have bitter, resentful children. So much resource is spent on producing athletic stars.

What's the percentage of kids who will end up in the pros anyway? Even if they do, they often self-destruct. Is there any million-dollar athletic personality whom you would want your kids to be like? If you and your husband haven't heard from God Himself to support such extracurricular pursuits for your kids, stop pouring time and money down a black hole.

Forming Your Filter

Let me share with you some values that we hold as non-negotiable in our home. Perhaps some will summon convictions residing in your heart that may have been suppressed by the busyness of life and the prevailing trends of our culture. These are some of the building blocks of our family's kingdom filter. If you'd like to read more specifics on any of these topics, along with other subjects of interest, please note the appendix entitled "The ABCs of Practical Parenting" at the back of the book.

- Every family member in our household is fully committed to our local church. Each of us plays a vital role in the life of the body.
- Attitude is almost everything at our house.
- Bored kids will meet with hard work.
- Household chores are an integral part of character training and development for our children.
- Electronic amusements are apportioned by parents with strict time allotments usually as an earned privilege. This includes video games, computer play, e-mail, instant messaging, web browsing, movies, and television viewing.
- Punks only have entrance for evangelistic purposes as determined by a parent.
- Girls don't call our boys without permission from Mom.
- Greeting adults enthusiastically and with proper social etiquette is not optional.
- Junk food won't build healthy bodies. Wholesome food predominates in our pantry.
- Happy kids are not our goal.
- Unusual manners should be the norm for our children.
- Kittens, puppies, and other pets are not a given at our house.
- We refuse to be mall rats.
- Cell phones are not necessarily standard equipment for children of any age.
- Television has its place in our kingdom homes; the closet works really well most of the time!

- Our children must learn to zip their lips at times in order to master that restless muscle of the tongue.
- Written communication such as thank-you notes are not an optional task for our children.
- Overnights at others' homes are a rarity for our kids.
- Movies for our children's viewing must have parental approval in selection and timing.
- Reading good books is a priority for us.
- Bedrooms in our home will not be decorated with suggestive or scary posters.
- "Yes, sir" or "yes, ma'am" are appropriate responses for kids to learn to say to elders.
- Pouting and whining are unacceptable behaviors for our children.
- Siblings will love each other in our home whether they like it or not.
- Counting to three and sentencing our kids to time-outs doesn't teach our children quick obedience or respect for authority.
- Computers with internet access are not allowed in our sons' bedrooms.
- Entertainment will not be excessively indulged in by our boys.
- Televisions cannot be found in any of our children's bedrooms.
- Puppy love is what happens when I take my young men to the pet store. Period.
- Outdoor play stimulates creativity and provides hours of physical exercise necessary to build healthy kids, so it's not an optional activity at our house.

This isn't a comprehensive list of our values, but it offers at least a peek into how we function in our home. By no means perfect, yet sincere in our endeavors, God is giving us good results due in large part to our commitment to these very practical values which we see supported by the Bible. It's not what's "meant to be" that determines the outcome of our kid's lives, but rather our practical strategies implemented through our daily choices in life.

The proof of the pudding is in the eating, as the ol' saying goes. Could it be time to change the recipe at your house?

CHAPTER ELEVEN

Refuse to Be a Victim!

The only easy day was yesterday.
—Unknown

I've heard it said that in life, we all must make the best of a bad situation. I completely agree. None of us begins with a clean slate. Life isn't what we see in the magazines and movies, as much as we'd like it to be. Each of us is born to imperfect parents with an already flawed set of circumstances. This fact of life is a part of the human condition. Don't be tempted to think others have it easier. God knows the particular challenges each of us have been handed in life.

Instead of playing beggar, waiting for a hand-out, or envying those around you who have more, begin to use what meager things you have in your hand. It's not important what's *in* your hand, but rather what you're *doing* with what's in your hand. By investing the little you have today, kingdom principles take over. Before you know it, what started out as insignificant begins to grow and multiply. Resources increase, relationships occur, and supernatural forces kick in, defying our natural limitations.

Consider Moses' folks; *they used what they had* to save their child instead of bemoaning their meager resources. Push had come to shove when these low-income parents found themselves stuck between a rock and a hard place. My husband says that most heroes aren't born, they're cornered. I think that theory must have applied to this now-famous, expectant couple, Amram and Jochebed. Living in Egypt and hearing of Pharaoh's latest edict, they could have fretted and freaked out with worry and high-powered anxiety upon the birth of a *son*. But they refused to be victims.

Cornered as they were, Amram and Jochebed proved to be heroes of faith who were unwilling to live by the nightly news reports. They believed in a sovereign God who was bigger than any natural limitations. They chose to be *no ordinary parents*. They were looking for what no man could give them, safe passage for their son. This determined, faith-filled, and probably desperate mother and father started their revolution with a basket made of reeds and mud—stuff within their reach. *God met them at the end of their natural resources* and transcended their meager offerings with His perfect provision.

> **They chose to be *no ordinary parents*.**

What's in Your Hands?

Life is verifiably hard and training children is a challenge, and there have been days, honestly, when I felt like giving in, resigning, wanting to say, "I can't! I quit!" But the Scriptures kept contradicting what my emotions were feeling. This haunting verse I mentioned earlier from 2 Peter 1:3 always reminds me, *His divine power has given us everything we need for life and godliness through our knowledge of him who called us by his own glory and goodness. Everything* is pretty comprehensive!

So many parents remain poor and wretched and blind and naked for lack of tapping into greater stores locked up in heavenly places by denying the truth of what's *already in their hands*. They're too busy coveting what they perceive are their neighbors' better resources. In Jesus' parable of the ten talents, we see this principle in action. Luke 19:26 says, *He replied, "I tell you that to everyone who has, more will be given, but as for the one who has nothing, even what he has will be taken away."* Use what's in your hands!

This can seem upside down, backwards, and unjust to our human thinking, but in God's economy, it is a principle of "use it or lose it." This concept may even offend you, but if it does, remember: revelation often comes through the door of offense. Don't harden your heart. Let truth have its perfect work in you. What secrets lie in obedience! Oh what infinite heavenly treasure chests await our movement toward God!

The key to obtaining more is to use what He's already given you, no matter how small. How you live *today* determines how you and your children will live *tomorrow*. You have the privilege of writing your own future, to a large degree. You want to be a ten-talent family in the future? Prove this by how you live as a one-talent man or woman in the now. Plant that measly little seed and watch it flourish! God visits our frail, practical, human steps and transforms them into the quantum leaps we've only dreamed of!

Look at what *is* there, rather than what is *not* there. For instance:

• What are we doing with the influence we have in our kids' lives?

- What are we doing with the hours of our life?
- What are we doing with our Bibles and our prayer lives?
- What are we doing with the time we spend with our children?
- What are we doing with the diet we are feeding our families?
- What are we doing with our computers and televisions and DVD players?
- What are we doing with the local church we attend?

Every resource we've got is meant to be a tool to aid us in the battle for the hearts of our children. Victim days are over. *Don't allow the enemy to box you in* based on what's in your wallet, how you lived your yesterdays, the present condition of your children, your address, the opinions of men or any other present circumstance. We must refuse to be victims

> **How you live *today* determines how you and your children will live *tomorrow*.**

of our circumstances. Write it down, tack it up on the frig and live by it! *Don't lie against the truth of God's promised provision. You have every single thing you need today, in your hands, for successfully parenting world-changers.*

Perhaps in the past you've felt like the needy man in Acts 14, always watching everyone else being blessed, waiting for the crumbs to fall into his hands. But it's a new day, and I believe God would say to you, "Stand up on your feet!" Read on.

Acts 14:8–10 tells the story: *In Lystra there sat a man crippled in his feet, who was lame from birth and had never walked. He listened to Paul as he was speaking. Paul looked directly at him, saw that he had faith to be healed and called out, "Stand up on your feet!" At that, the man jumped up and began to walk.*

Perhaps you've been "lame from birth" in your mind-set about God's provision. Let the Holy Spirit change you *even now*. There is a time to weep and mourn and cry out for the actual, living now-portion which you need. Then, march on and proceed in great faith!

Expect a Battle

Victory is our only option. We must not accommodate failure in our theology. I'm convinced we parents need to wake up in the morning with the gloves on! You will not just "get" good kids. You won't "fall" into a good mood each day. Face it. You will never simply *slide* into victory.

For those of you who feel you've lost ground to the enemy, expect opposition as you begin to take back the ground you've lost. You must *expect a battle* at every turn when you are trying to walk in the fullness of all God has for you and your household. 1 Peter 4:12

reminds us, *Do not be surprised at the painful trial you are suffering as though something strange were happening to you.* Too many of us Christians are spiritual and emotional weaklings who, at the slightest sign of resistance, cave in.

How do I know? Because I've done it! But these are days which demand our vigor, moral strength, and fortitude! Jude 1:3 exhorts us to be fighters: *I felt I had to write and urge you to contend for the faith that was once for all entrusted to the saints.* The prize we're striving for will go to those who are willing to box for it. We must allow God to give us a combative, pugnacious spirit against opposing spiritual enemies and their vile threats, in order to attain what He promises us.

> **We must allow God to give us a combative, pugnacious spirit against opposing spiritual enemies and their vile threats, in order to attain what He promises us.**

You must stand on God's Word, believing and fighting for what He wants to give you. Ephesians 6:12 says: *We do not wrestle against flesh and blood, but against principalities, against powers, against the rulers of the darkness of this age, against spiritual hosts of wickedness in the heavenly places* (NKJV).

Women, this includes you! If you're not wrestling today, I can guarantee you're on a downhill slide. I don't care if it was the prophet of all prophets who spoke over your life, you will have to fight on your knees, every day, for that word to come to pass in your life and in the lives of your children. You're not automatically going to have godly little children following you around like signs and wonders. My five sons are the first thing I pray for every single day. We must be absolutely indefatigable in this battle! If you're not contending, then you are certainly not going to win.

A Sovereign Plan, Lacking Nothing

I remember sitting on my bed, convinced my children were lacking. Our relationships with other young families seemed to be few and far between during this desert patch in our lives. My husband and I had recently suffered a severe job-related setback and found ourselves at the mercy of God with four little boys, a new baby, and no steady income. It was humbling. Those were days when we didn't have money for music lessons, furnishings, or other luxuries.

One rather affluent couple with whom we enjoyed a friendship seemed to have the best of everything: designer house complete with all the accoutrements desired for growing kids, remote-controlled vehicles the little ones could drive, trampoline, private pool, bikes and trails to ride them on, lessons of every kind, and organized sports' teams to enjoy. Pondering our plight one day, I sat alone on my bed and cried, lamenting our lot.

We were stuck and determined not to take the credit card escape hatch. We had to build an altar during that time, crying out to God for help. But the voices in Egypt kept calling, "Your kids need this and that, and they need it *now*."

Now as I look back, I see that God chose to give my boys the better things in life. I was thinking in the slums. God was thinking of His glory. Now I see His glory in each of our son's lives. Our Father in heaven knew in His wisdom that the qualities I had so longed to see in my boys were not going to come with a life of ease and pleasure.

> **No matter what our difficult circumstances, disadvantages, or limitations may try to shout at us, we must side with God and believe His Word!**

My problem is that sometimes I've looked at what others have had in their hands and moaned about what I lack. You might have done the same. Have these thoughts crossed your mind? Perhaps *"She* has very involved and caring relatives who regularly shoulder the load of her children." And, *"They* may have unlimited funds for lessons, lavish vacations, and edu-toys." Or, *"Others* may have the perfect charter school for their kids." It doesn't matter. Our kids weren't given to "she," "they," or "others." They were given to us. No matter what our difficult circumstances, disadvantages, or limitations may try to shout at us, we must side with God and believe His Word!

Philippians 4:19 tells us that *My God will meet all your needs according to his glorious riches in Christ Jesus.* I am convinced that my God will supply what I need, but perhaps not everything I *think* I need or want. We must choose to believe all that is *necessary* for the preparation and training of our kids will be there for us at the right time.

CHAPTER TWELVE

We Live by Faith!

Without faith it is impossible to please God.
                            —Hebrews 11:6

There is nothing natural in me that can raise a good kid. The Word of God says that in my flesh *dwells no good thing* (Romans 7:18, NKJV). I am dependent on God to achieve anything good in my parenting. Psalms 16:2 confirms that fact. *You are my Lord; apart from you I have no good thing.* The power to raise leaders has to come from deliberate, active, day-at-a-time faith in God. Without faith it is impossible to please God and I'm persuaded that without faith it is impossible to raise extraordinary kids! *Real faith demands works to become legitimate.* Moses' parents were facing life-or-death issues. What did they do? They listened for God's voice with a heart full of faith, they expected a miracle, and *they got busy!* God does not answer emotion. He answers faith, and *faith is demonstrated by works.*

Feelings

Many people *feel* a lot. The problem comes when they think *feeling* is the same as *doing.* They *strongly feel* the desire to raise godly children. *They are convinced* they don't want average kids. Most parents I know would be *deeply sorrowful* if their sons and daughters took a wrong path, married an unsuitable partner, or went astray. We have lots of emotional people all over the globe who aren't having an impact in their childrearing. They fuss, freak, whine, and nag all day, but God hasn't taken notice. His Word clearly says, *Faith without works is dead* (James 2:26, NKJV). He notices and answers *faith* that is measured by *action.*

Action is when you wake an hour early to pray for the outcome of your son or daughter's life, interceding for their choice of friends, prospective spouse, life's calling, financial affairs, fighting for their very destiny. Action is when you begin to implement all the things God is teaching you as you pursue wisdom from the Word and from others regarding your children and your home life. These are practical acts of faith which guarantee God's response.

Prayer

As people of faith, let's take stock of our prayer life. We parrot the phrase, "Christianity is not a religion; it is a relationship." How then do we differ from unbelievers if we don't spend time relating to the One with whom we claim to have a relationship? Are we living "religion" or are we living the truth?

> **Where are we in our lives with God? I want to urge us on to greater things.**

Where are we in our lives with God? I want to urge us on to greater things.

Over the years, I have sat with mothers who have raised godly children, and I have begged them for insight into how their sons and daughters became great men and women. Time and again, their answer has simply been prayer, prayer, and more prayer. Mary Queen of Scots said this: "I fear the prayers of John Knox more than all the armies of England." Even a sovereign queen, a woman of nobility and natural power, understood the supernatural power of prayer. The question is, "Do we?"

What's Your Plumb Line?

What's the cause of all the worldliness, powerlessness, and ineffectiveness in our homes? That's easy: wrong plumb lines. We feed on secular, humanistic idealism every time we view the news, read the paper, or study college-level academics at most universities. We feast on fashion, entertainment, food, recreation, and assorted frivolity while perusing the latest magazines. We ingest massive portions of convincing, demonic philosophies in the movies we're renting, yet we wonder why our daily lives are askew.

What is your measure of success, happiness, failure, beauty, or achievement? Are you perpetually discontented, disillusioned, bored, irritable, broke, worn-out, and disappointed? What, in actual fact, are you building? If your life and the lives of your children seem crooked, unstable, and weakly established, then trade in your old plumb line and seize the plumb line of God's Word! Get it out daily, measure your lives against it, and make the necessary adjustments to realign your family and set them on a new course of successful building.

If your children are turning heads for the wrong reasons in your community, I want to ask you, "What is your standard?" Is it *Self* magazine? Is it *In Style, People Magazine,* or *Sports Illustrated for Kids?* In what is your family marinating? What is it that you're embracing as your doctrine for life practice? Friends, we should be unceasingly occupied by the Word of God. If you're not seeing the kind of fruit you want to see in your children, hold up God's Word against your current methodology and see if perhaps you need to make some changes in order to realize the dreams you have for your kingdom kids.

Several years ago, I felt impressed to cut beauty and celebrity magazines out of my life. I thought flipping through these publications was just free time spent in the dentist's office, on the airplane, or in the check-out line. It's likely that a lot of you might feel the same about the remote control. We may use the phrase, "I'm just killing some time." I sensed the Holy Spirit saying that the time I was killing was killing me!

After making this tiny adjustment in my daily life, I replaced the junk with God's Word. I was amazed to see how the five minutes I thought I would be reading turned into twenty, thirty, or more. That's a whole bunch of seed sown added up over the years, whether for good or not-so-good. I noted that after a year's time, three years' time, and more, my mind-set, my aspirations, my focus was being purified. Cut off what's unhelpful. Replace it with what's lasting.

The Only Plumb Line We Can Trust

Hebrews 1:3 tells us that *He sustains all things by His powerful Word.* This truth motivates me! We think we need so many things to sustain our lives and the lives of our kids that we can neglect this boulder of truth. It's not *stuff* we need! It is God's Word we need! The Bible is not some ancient, meaningless book of empty words. It is the power of God unto salvation!

Sustain is a powerful word with comprehensive meaning. Its definition implies support, strength, comfort, and encouragement. According to this, God's Word will uphold, confirm, bring permanence to, and enable withstanding, bearing up, and enduring. Apply each of these terms to your situation. What strength you are promised by His Word!

> **The Bible is not some ancient, meaningless book of empty words. It is the power of God unto salvation!**

So what are we thinking by spiritually starving ourselves first and then our children, yet expecting to raise strong leaders? In five, ten, fifteen years some of you may be whining, "But God, I served you and raised my children to serve you, and now Susie's married to a loser, Junior is a homosexual, . . . yakity, yakity yak . . . Poor me; it's all Your fault God." But in actual fact, these unfortunate developments will be due to malnutrition. It would be considered abuse if you didn't give your children physical food. But since it's only the Bread of Life, or merely the sovereign Maker of the universe . . . well, aw shucks, who will know any better if I just live off the crumbs from my Promise Box, rather than feasting from the entire Bible?

Let me tell you who knows: The devil knows and the spiritual powers in high places and the angels all know. And in the end, the culmination of your child's destiny will be determined, to a large degree, by the impartation, or lack of, this necessary nutrient of the Word of God. When many parents come before the living God, the Creator of all mankind, to answer for how they handled their infinitely precious blessings called children, their knees will buckle. They will be without defense because they neglected the holy discipline of instilling the Word of God into their children.

The Anointing of God

We need an anointing to raise godly children! 1 John 2:27 says, *As for you, the anointing you received from him remains in you, and you do not need anyone to teach you. But as his anointing teaches you about all things and as that anointing is real, not counterfeit—just as it has taught you, remain in him.*

Let's depend on the Holy Spirit, and expect His anointing to teach us how to parent. We can buy books on how to raise kids and many times just find a legalistic set of rules. So when we've followed all the rules and the results are disappointing, we blame God or the book. No, no, no. You tried it the wrong way. It starts down on your knees where you receive an anointing from the living God. I picture myself in prayer, making a divine exchange. Trading my better ideas, my human reasoning, my secular standards, my friends' advice, for a heavenly anointing that enables me to succeed. We cannot parent effectively without the anointing of God.

- I need an anointing to know whether to say "yes" or "no" to my kids.
- I need an anointing to know how to speak into their lives.
- I need an anointing to know what friends they're to play with.
- I need an anointing to know where to take them in this world.
- I need an anointing to train them how to spend their money.
- I need an anointing to protect them in this hour.

Don't ignore the promptings in your spirit. If you have committed your life to Jesus Christ, then the Holy Spirit is living in you, and He will stir you to action if you'll be sensitive to Him. Those leadings are the weapons that God is giving you. In the meantime, speak and prophesy by faith over your children. Preach to them, and give wisdom to them. Tell them the good you see in them. Tell them God is for them, and He has great things in store for them, even while you firmly impose the guardrails God gives you around their young lives.

Faith Expressed

Faith enables me to persevere in child training.

- **By faith I see my vision before me**! Godly men and women leading in their generation.
- **By faith I encourage myself daily**! I remind myself out loud of "who I really am" in this world, beyond the dirty toilets, toy-strewn living room, and sleepless nights of teething babies, which may be my current reality. Even though I may feel like a nobody at times, I remind myself that I am a powerful weapon in God's hand, used to shape and sharpen these vessels. Beyond my immediate roles of nanny, cook, housekeeper, and nurse, I lift my gaze to the reality of my true identity in Christ in this season—revolutionary, history-maker, world-changer, and above all, nurturer of young men of God. I remind myself that my days are numbered. I remind myself that this world needs a deliverer. I remind myself that the weapons for producing deliverers are *in my hands*.

> Beyond my immediate roles of nanny, cook, housekeeper, and nurse, I lift my gaze to the reality of my true identity in Christ in this season—revolutionary, history-maker, world-changer, and above all, nurturer of young men of God.

- **By faith I speak over my sons**! I tell them, "You are called to be a leader. You are head and shoulders above the crowd, and to whom much is given, much is required. Don't forget, there's a very high call on your life." We must remind our kids of their remarkable potential from the time they're born. I don't care if they've just been given the grounding of their life for being caught in a convoluted scheme with a friend. As I said, I am speaking by faith which is *the assurance of things hoped for, the conviction of things not seen* (Hebrews 11:1, RSV).

With a particular son of mine who always seemed to be pushing the envelope, I would begin with something like this: "Son, I am your biggest fan. I love you and I am committed to you. I know you are destined to be a general for God. You have an amazing call on your life; I see it all over you. Remember those prophetic promises?! I wholeheartedly disagree with what you did, and you'll be grounded for at least a month, but I am telling you, you are a giant, the world is going to know your name someday, and you are going to change nations."

> **Faith in God's unseen reality always surpasses what is actually before my eyes.**

Michelangelo saw David in that renowned rock. You may look at your son or daughter and think, "He's just a rock." "He's not special." I urge you: seek, seek, seek what God has put into his substance, and you will find, find, find great treasure and success! Shape it, chisel it, and speak by faith into it! Faith in God's unseen reality always surpasses what is actually before my eyes.

- **By faith I speak of them and the greatness of God in them**! I boast of their greatness at every possible chance. I'm not endorsing arrogant chatter about their frivolous strengths, like appearance, sports' skills, etc., but sober evaluation of and gratitude for their God-given assets. Behind the rough and tumble, bickering with brothers, bombing on a test, or an occasional acne-sprinkled exterior, is a human being with a tremendous future. I'm talking about turn-the-world-upside-down capability. Their enormous capacity for leadership is being developed. I recite these truths out loud to myself and, at times, to others. All my boys are brilliant, no matter what they got on their report cards or what temporary misconduct may be staring me in the face.

At the beach I saw a gal who was dragging her screaming child by the arm across the sand. The mom was beside herself with emotion, shrieking, "Oh, why were you born! I can't stand you! I wish I could leave you here." I'm sure she didn't know she was speaking words of death over her daughter's life. Proverbs 18:21 tells us, *The tongue has the power of life and death.* I believe words are power tools—use them with wisdom!

Ugly words shouldn't echo off the walls of our homes. I don't care how naughty or raucous our children are. We should never say, "You embarrass me, you little brat!" We say, "You are amazing. You are outstanding! Look at what God has given you! Are you going to squander it on that stupid situation? You're going to lose your voice in the kingdom just so you can enjoy that pleasurable sin!? Forget it! You're not going to get away with that as long as I have anything to do with it. You have too high a calling to do that."

Friends, we have to speak *by faith* when we don't see the promises, because faith focuses on *what we don't see.* We see it right here in our heart, and we know it to be true in our spirit. We see that strength in our kids. We see that compassionate heart. We see that discernment. We see that intolerance for evil and that love for the Word.

We've got to bless what we see by speaking affirming words. We've got to speak it over them, loud and clear.

- **By faith I speak to the mountains in my life!** Jesus said, *If you have faith as small as a mustard seed, you can say to this mountain, "Move from here to there" and it will move. Nothing will be impossible for you* (Matthew 17:20). I take Him at His Word! I believe we should confess aloud so all the powers that be can hear us! My husband will often ask me when I'm in the kitchen cleaning up, "What are you muttering about?" I'll say, "I'm not muttering; I'm confessing." I'm speaking to mountains. I'm telling that mountain to be removed. I'm confessing resolution to that conflict in our home. I'm commanding that rebellion in our teenager, or perhaps that rebellion in me, to be gone! "Down with you!" I declare by faith.

- **By faith I protect my children when speaking of them to others.** If somebody comes up and says, "Oh I heard what happened with Junior," in a that's-just-too-bad tone, I'll respond candidly, "You know it is, but it's a learning experience. Junior's going to grow through this, and he's going to become a mighty man. I see such greatness in him. He's a general, you know. One day he's going to lead multitudes to Jesus." Don't ever allow a coercive inquiry to make you bad-mouth your kids out of a sense of inferiority. I fight with my mouth; I fight with my prayers; I fight with my life.

> **I fight with my mouth; I fight with my prayers; I fight with my life.**

Pay the Price in Persevering Prayer

What is the price we must pay? We must pay with persevering prayers. We cannot pray half-hearted, lukewarm prayers, but heartfelt, impassioned, prayers. Token prayers will never be enough to break down sinful patterns and break into frontiers of the supernatural realm! It is the unwavering, Pit-Bull prayers which come from God and His Word, wrestling in the night and refusing to surrender any hope, faith, or promise. This prayerful posture is not ambivalence, passing fancy, emotionalism, or daydreams. No, this is real. This is time-consuming, meaty stuff.

Psalms 127:1 warns us as parents, *Unless the Lord builds the house, its builders labor in vain.* Let's not be those who labor in vain. Believe with me this verse we sing:

My hope is built on nothing less
Than Jesus' blood and righteousness;
I dare not trust the sweetest frame,
But wholly lean on Jesus' name.
On Christ the solid Rock I stand.

All other ground is sinking sand.
All other ground is sinking sand.

Live on your knees for your kids. What price is too high to pay for our sons and daughters? So many want to reap a harvest of righteousness, to make huge withdrawals from the heavenly account toward their succeeding generations, but they're unwilling to make sufficient deposits to meet those ends. Are you praying? "Well . . ." comes a faltering reply. Are you in the Word? "Well . . ." comes another hesitant response.

I pray, "Oh God, forgive us our lies against You. *How hard we've worked at perfecting mediocrity!* How we've invested in temporal things and forgotten to store up treasures in heaven! How long we've labored for stuff that doesn't last! How we've churned out protégés of pathetic religious form, instead of disciples of Jesus Christ, and Pharisees of legalistic labors, instead of humble, serving kingdom builders. Oh God, forgive our sins of lust, greed, gluttony, hoarding, control, rebellion, lack of forgiveness, malice, fits of rage, arrogance—all our fleshly ways of thinking and living. Oh God, forgive us. Cleanse us by the blood of Jesus. Change us that we might be vessels fit for preparing the next generation of kingdom leaders."

> **How hard we've worked at perfecting mediocrity!**

84

CHAPTER THIRTEEN

Don't Say "Peace" When God Says "War!"

What makes us Christians shrug our shoulders when we ought to be flexing our muscles? What makes us apathetic in a day when there are loads to lift, a world to be won, and captives to be set free? Why are so many bored when the times demand action?
—Billy Graham

A s I read Jeremiah 6:14–19, I knew God was speaking something important to me. I was especially drawn to verse fourteen: *They dress the wound of my people as though it were not serious. "Peace, peace," they say, when there is no peace.* To make light of a deadly physical wound in our children would be unthinkable. Nothing would stop us from getting urgent care! We would dial 911 without a second thought. We must approach the spiritual wound afflicting so many children of this generation with the very same urgency! We can't be relaxed while the destiny of our children is hanging in the balance. Don't make peace when God says, "Make war!"

Joel 3:9 says, *Proclaim this among the nations: Prepare for war! Rouse the warriors! Let all the fighting men draw near and attack.* Where are the fighting men, women, and children? So many people in our day prefer peace. It's pleasant, calm, and quiet. Peace is preferable, but *often peace can only be found on the other side of war*. Parents who love peace to a fault must allow God to give them a will to war for their children. Our world today is a minefield, and our kids' lives are at stake.

It's time you make war on the circumstances in your kid's life with which you aren't at peace. We must take the battle to the very gates if we intend to wage war effectively for our sons and daughters. These gates are the *points of entry* into their lives, including media, friends, school, "fun," cell phones, web exposure, entertainment, to mention a few. We will not live at peace with predators who lay in wait at these gates to our children's lives. I will slay every enemy that pokes its nose through the border of my rightful, God-given territory.

I begin the attack by wrestling and doing violence on my knees, and then I take action. We come out of the prayer closet and boldly refuse to coexist with rebellion, lust, greed, girlfriends, boyfriends, questionable parties, normalcy, teenage syndrome, fashion compulsion, surf culture, our own kid's laziness, R-rated movies, internet addiction, tabloid reading habits, and whatever else is infecting them.

> **I will slay every enemy that pokes its nose through the border of my rightful, God-given territory.**

We will not sip our coffee and play solitaire while we rent a room in our homes for rebellion to run wild! We will oust these insidious enemies from their nesting places. If necessary, we will turn our homes upside down to dislodge these vile snakes from their dens of hiding.

What's happening at home while you're out enjoying life or working that second job? Where are the children? One young man in Arizona had in his bedroom a large quantity of legally prescribed drugs for depression, along with marijuana and 151-proof rum. With his live web camera rolling and onlookers cheering and jeering, he proceeded to kill himself on a mixture of drugs and alcohol. Meanwhile, Mom sat in the next room doing crossword puzzles. Did these parents not know that while their son lived under their roof, they had control over every corner of that bedroom?

A worldly mind-set tells us we don't have the ability to step into our kids' lives and say, "I'm here to take over. I'm here to teach you a better way. I'm here to disciple you. I'm here to model what a godly man or woman is." This is faulty thinking. How does a twenty-one-year-old young man of promise, gifting, and possibility commit suicide with his mother in the room next door, playing a game? Let me tell you, and then together let us shout it from the roof tops: WE'VE MADE PEACE WHEN GOD SAYS MAKE WAR!

Be Ruthless with Sin

Jesus Christ is ruthless with sin. He said this in Mark 9:43–47, *"If your hand causes you to sin, cut it off. It is better for you to enter life maimed than with two hands to go into hell, where the fire never goes out. And if your foot causes you to sin, cut it off. It is better for you to enter life crippled than to have two feet and be thrown into hell. And if your eye causes you to sin, pluck it out. It is better for you to enter the kingdom of God with one eye than to have two eyes and be thrown into hell."*

What harsh words from our loving Savior! We forget that great love brings with it clear boundaries and great responsibility. Jesus knows the power of sinful patterns of behavior which remain unchecked in our lives. If we tolerate sinful patterns of behavior in our lives and in the lives of our children, we are inviting, as it were, a permanent dwelling for snakes. Snakes have babies. They multiply very quickly. We must be brutal and unyielding. We must annihilate them at once, because *what we tolerate, soon will dominate.*

My husband and I will remind each other of this principle as we're dealing in our home with our sons. The wrong attitudes, responses, and sinful indulgences we allow to remain and multiply in our sons' lives will prove to be deadly vipers both to the boys and to our household! In the spiritual realm, how many of us mothers and fathers have not only allowed, but fed, watered, and protected such "deadly reptiles" in our homes?

We must remind ourselves as discerning, spiritually keen parental authorities in our spheres that, in actual fact, we deserve what we tolerate. At those moments of realization in the face of battle, we must leave the bunker of our indecision and intimidation, resist the temptation to cower, and march back into the fray. We have to face any sinful expression we've allowed to wreak havoc in our homes: Make things right, untie that knot, straighten that arrow, polish that character, confront, and then slay that snake of sin. Then, we march right into the kitchen and make smoothies with our little soldiers! All in a day's work, fellow warriors. This is real life on the home front.

Resignation

We as parents must never resign ourselves to giving up. We must never throw in the towel by displaying helpless inactivity on our battlefields. Apathetically squandering precious hours, trading e-mail spam when our children are living in darkness, is tantamount to indifference. We must refuse to make peace with any unacceptable condition in our children when God would tell us to make war against it. We must not allow darkness or pockets of darkness to dwell in our homes and lives. I have the power to rule and reign in my territory, and *I will take no prisoners.*

We, as the people of God, must take responsibility for the tragic consequences of our sleeping in peace, shopping 'til we drop, sipping our coffee and tea, and nursing a laissez-faire attitude, while our children die a slow death spiritually. God is not moved by feeble, religious gestures, and He is not winking at our silly ways. He is beating on our doors and calling us to war for our sons and daughters. We

> From this day forward, God is going to cause you to declare war on some things that you've made peace with in the past.

87

must fight in the country, in the city, in the suburbs, at the beach, at the mall, in our schools, and in our own front and back yards.

From this day forward, God is going to cause you to declare war on some things that you've made peace with in the past. Perhaps at one time you endeavored to hold your standards high, but somehow you've drifted back into the mainstream's lazy river, losing ground with your children. Maybe you experienced some setbacks, thus allowing disillusionment to get the best of you. Proverbs 13:12 says that *hope deferred makes the heart sick*.

However, the second part of that verse says, *But a longing fulfilled is a tree of life*. God wants you to experience the fulfillment of your longings for your children. But first you must choose to shift gears from cruiser to conqueror! Today I'm reminding you that you have the power to intercept and dismantle the enemy's strategy for your children. Parents, be ruthless with sin and the devil's maneuvers!

Demonic Aggressors

> **In our day, demonic aggressors are pursuing the next generation, our sons and daughters.**

In our day, demonic aggressors are pursuing the next generation, our sons and daughters. They have declared war on our kids. It's not that life is simply strewn about with potholes and a few land mines to avoid, but I believe with all my heart there are aggressive enemies on the forefront that are after my kids! Homosexuals are intent on capturing our sons and daughters. I said "intent," not mediocre, not neutral, but actively militant. These aren't just casual mishaps. These enemies are hungry predators. Pharaoh is still devouring young men in the twenty-first century. He still wants to destroy the seed, just as he wanted to kill the male Israelite children. His goal is to take out the head, the men. He wants your sons just as badly as he did back then.

Historically, during a time of war, it's simply not business as usual. Even now as America has been entangled in the battle in Iraq, life has changed for millions in this nation, as well as around the world. In a time of *spiritual* war against a nation's very soul, her children, it's imperative that greater measures be taken to protect them from the enemy. He is described as *a roaring lion looking for someone to devour* in 1 Peter 5:8.

However he can get them, the enemy will take your kids if you aren't on guard at your post, Dad and Mom. Sometimes it seems that the devil wants our kids worse than we want our kids. I won't take time to list the many and varied sinister subcultures who would love to count your kids as members. Some are boldly knocking on your child's door *even now*. Matthew 24:43 reminds us that *if the owner of the house had known at what time of night the thief was coming, he would have kept watch and would not have let his house be broken into.* Let's not be found sleeping on our watch. These are hostile enemies bent on destruction. I beg us, don't be polite to them. They're after our kids, and we better get serious.

Pushing the Battle to the Gate

Winston Churchill said, "If we don't put our foot on the egg, we shall have to chase the chicken around the world's barnyard." I apply this to parenting. I'm convinced that hordes of loving, caring, sincere parents miss the boat on this one. We struggle with being the "bad guy" and pushing the battle to the gate. War is ugly and unpopular. Maybe rebellion, a bad attitude, or a persistent character flaw has surfaced in our child. We will run five miles around "the issue" to avoid hitting the point where the battle is actually raging. We look for an escape rather than enduring an awkward or painful confrontation, so we'll change the subject.

We may negotiate with the smokescreen the kid builds for us. We deliberate and pacify when in actual fact we are neglecting to deal with the crucial issue at hand. We feign peace when truly there is no peace, and in the end, we multiply the problem and create more havoc and unrest.

Here's a common battleground you might recognize. We've just picked up Junior from day care after a long day at the office. He begins whining in the grocery store as we're frantically trying to grab something, anything, to throw together for supper. His discontent persists. We cheerfully announce, "Let's rent a movie after we're done shopping! Just help Mommy/Daddy get through the grocery store without any trouble, and we'll have a party tonight." Never mind the fact that most of Junior's life *is* a party with very little required of him much of the time and the fact that he won't appreciate this party any more than he has appreciated the other daily parties thrown for him. But for now, this bribery works wonders!

This promise relieves a bit of pressure for the next aisle of shopping *until* Junior sees a giant container of licorice ropes or a super-size box of Sponge Bob candy breakfast bops or whatever his wicked little heart desires. He subtly begins to pine for what he wants. He begins softly with a decent demeanor, but as you subtly resist or pretend to ignore his advances, his conduct begins to threaten your "peace."

The strength of his request increases along with his volume, and you strike yet another deal to pacify him once again. You've bought yourself just enough oxygen to get through the check-out line with a minimum of embarrassment and with the appearance that perhaps Mom or Dad *is* in charge! Then it's off to the video store to rent the movie he has neither earned nor deserves. Because of guilt and exhaustion and denial, this overworked parent has again reinforced many bad behaviors he/she did not have the courage to deal with head-on. Ever been there?

We, as the God-given authority in our homes, must use the word "no" strongly and calmly, giving our children the comfort and security of knowing that "no" means "no" without drama unfolding thereafter. If Junior whines, Junior will get to go to the bathroom or car with Mommy or Daddy, whichever is more private. Junior's behavior has guaranteed for him the stick on the rear, in order to remind him of what acceptable behavior is and is not.

Mom and Dad must win this fight and be courageous enough to stand firm for all the threats that lie ahead. We must draw the line and stand by the line, or the line will perpetually be moved by Junior, who is clever, gutsy, and strong. God has gifted him with these skills, and it's up to us to channel all that power toward the mark that Junior must hit in order to come into his full inheritance and be a world-changer. Ultimately, his outstanding character will have tremendous multiple impact on those around him and on his children and grandchildren one day. But for now, it's war!

Guarding Their Innocence

Don't apologize for being cautious with your kids on stuff like videos, overnights, and wrong relationships. Dr. James Dobson says, "More damage can be done in one day than can be repaired in a lifetime." We must be on our guard! Let God be the eyes in the back of your head! Listen to His promptings when you're feeling uneasy about social gatherings with peers and murky-sounding plans created by adolescents. Close the door to those mysterious overnight excursions when kids are thrown together for twenty-four hours without tight supervision.

We can't be casual about the devil's traps being set for our children. Ephesians 4:27 exhorts us, *Do not give the devil a foothold.* We would do well to heed this warning in 1 Peter 5:8: *Be self-controlled and alert. Your enemy the devil prowls around like a roaring lion looking for someone to devour.* Refuse to live at ease, leaving your children unprotected and vulnerable. Those primary influences in their lives must be good and godly sources.

Take your place, and strongly lead these impressionable children! Place the boundaries where God leads you to place them, even when your decisions are extremely unpopular with your kids. Exert a lot of control in the early years and less control later on in order to *carefully* train your children according to Deuteronomy 11. Err on the side of caution if your spirit is raising red flags about anything to do with your youngsters. We

> **Take your place, and strongly lead these impressionable children!**

parents are the gate-keepers of our kids' lives for a very brief period of time. We must be vigilant. Lot led his family into Sodom, and then he couldn't get them out. It was *too late*. The hook was in.

CHAPTER FOURTEEN

We Are the Models

Don't worry that children never listen to you; worry that they are always watching you.

—Robert Fulghum

e reproduce what we are in our kids. What we *live*, not what we *believe*, will come to life in them. Moses is an illustration of this principle:

- Just like his mom and dad, Moses lived by faith instead of by his five senses.
- Just like his mom and dad, Moses chose to please God by traveling upstream against the current, even to the point of disobeying the powers that be.
- Just like his mom and dad, he did not fear what the state would do to him; he feared God first.

Moses knew no lifestyle other than his upbringing of faith. His parents were unwilling to settle for the king's decree, the status quo, if you will. They modeled a lifestyle of living for a greater King, in a greater kingdom. What will be said of you? What are you choosing to be as a mom and as a dad?

Tell Me Again!

How many times had Moses listened to Miriam tell the story of how Father and Mother began to pray when they realized Mother was pregnant? The joy of her pregnancy had been threatened by Pharaoh's decree that every male child under the age of two years would be thrown into the Nile to die. For a time these parents pondered the horrific state of affairs, and at the end of the day, they chose not to allow dire circumstances to rule them and the children God gave them. They would not live in fear or be intimidated by such wickedness and tyranny. Countless times, Miriam would find her mother and father at the river, at the fire, in the bedroom, in the kitchen, fervently crying out to the living God for a plan of holy protection for this unborn child.

Miriam was sworn to secrecy, and Mother was careful to dress in such a way as to hide her pregnancy. Wisdom guided her every move, and faith drove her daily life up until the birth of this little one. Promise guarded their hearts from panic as they laid eyes on this newborn son. This was *no ordinary child* who nursed at her breast, who found sweet contentment in her arms. Nothing would harm this little wonder!

Time marched on, and one day Miriam noticed Mother gathering reeds, drying them in the sun, and knotting them together to form a large, oblong basket. A strategy was taking shape. A practical plan was unfolding. As Mother and Father carefully, so carefully, perfected the sealing of every fiber with their clay mixture, they told Miriam of the grand scheme about to take place.

Mother nursed little Moses one last time, and the family prayed together with father leading. Then they placed the infant on the soft fabric lining in the basket and sealed the lid snugly on top. Mother was trying to hide her pain and her tears as she placed the basket in the reeds which grew along the Nile, running quickly back home to Father.

Miriam had been charged with watching the basket from a concealed spot behind a nearby tree. Before long, a cluster of women came along, giggling and chattering as they walked. Miriam could not believe her eyes. Frantic, she felt her knees weaken and the blood rush through her beating heart. Perfume wafted through the air amidst the unmistakable markings of a princess and her attendants. All of them wore garments of distinction and heavy make-up, and the dutiful handmaidens carried palms to shield the princess from the sun. But what of baby Moses . . . please God . . . mercy, oh Lord. Then suddenly little Moses began to wail!

Miriam thought she would faint as he drew the attention of this band of women. The leader, obvious royalty and perhaps the very daughter of Pharaoh, sent her servant to pull the floating basket to shore. She lifted the lid of the basket and let out a compassionate cry as she "oohed" and "aahed" over this child. Miriam found herself powerfully pulled to her feet by strong instinct. She presented herself to the princess and offered to find a nurse to feed the little one. As these events unfolded, it was as if she was still watching from a distance and something beyond her natural self was operating.

The princess agreed enthusiastically that a nurse was definitely needed and Miriam ran with all her energy back home to bring her mother the news. With Mother designated as the nursemaid, Miriam joyfully carried little Moses back to their home later that afternoon with the Princess' express permission. It was time for quiet celebration, awe, and wonder at the supernatural chain of events that had just taken place. This was more than a story; this was a bonafide miracle of enormous proportions that was remembered time and again quietly and aloud as the family praised God for His wonderful plan and protection.

How could Moses forget his roots? How could he think differently? Moses was the product of his parents' unwavering faith and unswerving commitment to a mighty God. His resolve was unshakable. He had no option but to do the same: trust in the Almighty all the days of his life.

> **Moses was the product of his parents' unwavering faith and unswerving commitment to a mighty God.**

Dwarfing Our Kids

God does not create ordinary children. It is parents who create ordinary children. Spiritually dull parents cannot see beyond the surface of things; they think too little of their offspring and unknowingly dwarf their children's destinies with small mindedness, tiny faith, and no vision. In the words of A.T. Robertson, "More children are cursed into the world than blessed, because of the parents they were given."

I'm deeply distressed as I ponder the waste of substance never carefully considered, measured, and combined to create a successful end product called a child. How troubling to survey the discombobulated result, so dwarfed by the clumsy, foolish hands of sincere, but not devout parents! Anguish fills my soul as I surmise what may result. What fruit is yet to be born by such a youngster? I can't help but imagine his life is a seedbed of sin and troubles galore, just waiting to manifest. Are you dwarfing the destinies of your children by the way you live your life? We've got to come to the table with something more than what we're asking from them. We've got to practice what we preach.

Out of the Mouths of Babes

We cry, "Oh God, we want our kids to be deliverers!" But what are we? We are establishing the standard, casting the mold, and that's serious stuff. We can preach it down, but if we aren't living it, kids know it. You can't get anything past them. They call a spade a spade, and whether I like it or not, sometimes I'm the spade! When they critique me, I listen, even when it hurts, and nine times out of ten my kids are right. I may have been home schooling them for the better part of twenty years, but it sure seems like they've been teaching me!

Bill Gates says, "Your most unhappy customers are your greatest source of learning." We can learn a whole lot if we listen to our critics. If we let them, our children can be a rich source of information for us. Just as we want our kids to adjust themselves, we have to adjust ourselves and allow our character issues to be confronted in a loving and respectful way. Are we too proud or insecure to receive truth from our children?

My boys can tell you about my weaknesses: how I've failed and all the times I've had to say "I'm sorry." I say, "Boys, tell me the hard stuff." I hate it, but I have to hear it because my kids see the real me. They see my idiosyncrasies, and they see my layers that need to come off. They don't use it as a bargaining chip or a deflecting measure if I'm exhorting them in an area, but they know they can say anything to me if they say it in respect.

We have to lay down old wives' tales and ancient, unhelpful traditions and have teachable hearts when our kids approach us. Remember, we're modeling what they will become, and we want them to relate to their children in a real way. If there are relational issues between my boys and me then I must consider if what I'm blaming on them is perhaps a reflection of me. I think it is a safe place to live when Mom and Dad can be respectfully approached about anything.

Parents who desire their kids to soar, best not be limping along themselves. Your children are watching you. Luke 6:39 says, *Can a blind man lead a blind man? Will they not both fall into a pit? A student is not above his teacher but everyone who is fully trained, will be just like his teacher*. What are you? If you want giants for kids who go miles ahead of you, then you better start running after every single thing you want for them! As parents, the onus rests upon us. We must be able to say to our children, "Follow me as I follow Christ. I am an example to you of how to live this kingdom life on earth." We want to feel them nipping at our heels, and when we do, we better take another leap forward!

> **Parents who desire their kids to soar, best not be limping along themselves.**

CHAPTER FIFTEEN

Hey, Mom and Dad: You're the Experts!

*Take at hazard one hundred children of several educated generations and one hundred uneducated children of the people and compare them in anything you please; in strength, in agility, in mind, in the ability to acquire knowledge, even in morality—**and in all respects you are startled by the vast superiority on the side of the children of the uneducated.***

—Count Leo Tolstoy, Education and Children (1862)

I am not a system chick. I don't like the system and the system doesn't like me. I'm suspicious of organizations with fancy names boasting expert panels that disseminate advice on nutrition, childhood vaccinations, education, and many other topics regarding "healthy child development," as they call it. We agree to disagree on many issues. I wish everyone loved me, but it seems like so many of my beliefs crash headlong into their beautiful fantasies. Every time I've tried to hold hands with Egypt, I find myself compromising my core convictions.

One fall I enrolled my children in a government-funded home school program in order to get high school credits. The ongoing battle I faced with the administration week after week, spending hours wrestling with my appointed supervisor over what education is and isn't, became such a distraction and so emotionally exhausting I decided to live without the credits.

In reality, it's a futile effort to attempt to be acceptable to such secular establishments because we will never be able to mesh with systems motivated by humanism when we are motivated by the living God. We are in direct opposition to one another from the foundation up! We can be polite, but we will never see eye-to-eye. Eventually, we may even find ourselves going "nose-to-nose" over significant issues. Let me hasten to say that *we're never fighting against people.* According to Ephesians 6:12, *Our struggle is not against flesh and blood, but against the rulers, against the authorities, against the powers of this dark world and against the spiritual forces of evil in the heavenly realms.* Those spiritual forces can be intimidating.

As people of God, it's nigh impossible to be best friends with the "Pharaohs" of this age. If you're trying to do that, you're probably hiding who you really are and what you're all about because *who you really are and what you're all about is going to cut across the system.* Face it, in many instances your freedom will threaten their agenda. Be bold, and come to terms with this fact: We are not at peace with the system.

Private Pitfalls

Private systems aren't exempt from potential pitfalls, either. Any organization, once healthy and well-functioning, with *an established way of doing something,* can become rigid and unhelpful or even toxic. Take Christian schools, for instance. Those of us leading in such academies must ensure that legalism and religiosity don't creep in and shout more loudly than our claims to build character. Let's be discerning in our recruiting so our faculty isn't bulging with Pharisees who hold their students to one standard while they live another. God forbid that hypocrisy would smolder beneath the surface of our tidy Christian learning centers! Kids are no dummies. Only adults seem to brush over, ignore, or rationalize these crucial inconsistencies in their kids' mentors.

Let's not provide a stiff box for every student to fit into when in actuality only a rare few can truly conform. Let's not perpetuate a system which makes failures of kids who think they've lost when they haven't even had a chance to play the game. Let's guard against any sinful favoritism or blacklisting that originates in our deceitful hearts.

> **We must define for ourselves our goals in parenting and educating our children, explore all the available options, and use only those resources which we determine will enhance and support our God-given goals.**

Our goal must not be to produce perfect little specimens in their uniform uniforms, uniformly fitting into the uniform box prepared in the uniform setting of the average private school. My heart beats to see our children *unchained* from the restricted menu of the religious order. Their classroom should consist of wide open spaces where they are encouraged to find their unique expression within the freeing parameters of biblical values. They must be liberated to grow organically, running toward their destiny! I believe we can pursue these objectives even though our students may be wearing matching outfits. It's not about the garb, but about the heart and spirit of our mission as educators.

I don't want to raise spiritless kids with no backbone. Beware of school systems which in actual fact are crippling the kids they proclaim to be developing. We must not bow the knee to our modern-day Egypt. We must define for ourselves our goals in parenting and educating our children, explore all the available options, and use only those resources which we determine will enhance and support our God-given goals. We must reject whatever doesn't fit into our vision, even if "everyone" is doing it.

Experts

Systems are full of experts. What is a so-called expert in our day? Is he like the Wizard of Oz, who simply paralyzes others in fear and makes them feel like fools? Is she a scholarly individual with lots of letters behind her name and impressive tenure in the public school system, or is the expert perhaps an academic who spends life perpetually learning, but never able to come to a knowledge of the truth?

Any topic I see discussed on television, radio, and in magazines always seems to have an "expert" personality included as the final word on the subject. Most of these eggheads make me tired as they endlessly drone on. Someone has wisely noted, "We have experts everywhere who know more and more about less and less, until some of them know nearly everything about nothing."

> You are the true experts your kids need, gifted so by God, with or without a doctorate in higher education!

Don't get me wrong. Experts have their place. Give me an expert to fly the airplane I'm riding in or to set a broken bone or to repair my vehicle. They are worth their weight in gold when my internet is down, my washing machine is broken, or my power is out. I appreciate the scientific discoveries that have transformed our modern lives. But when it comes to most of the issues of childrearing, a Ph.D. is not the determining factor for expertise. We need the wisdom of the Maker of the universe, the Name above all Names, and He doesn't charge by the hour.

In the vast majority of matters pertaining to our children, I want to urge you, Mom and Dad: think for yourselves! No one but you owns your kids. Do what you determine is right for your children in accordance with God's Word and purposes for little Junior. You are the true experts your kids need, gifted so by God, with or without a doctorate in higher education! Let's tear the shroud of mystery off the lie called an "expert."

Permission to Parent

It seems to me that it has become politically incorrect to parent our children with clear, strong leadership. Why must we apologize for making unpopular decisions for our children as though it isn't our business to be deciding what's best for them? Parents and other adults seem almost afraid to take their God-given role as trainer, leader, model, and exhorter. This debilitating mind-set ought to be identified, repented of, and aborted from our modus operandi as parents. What nonsense we have accepted from this ungodly culture!

We call teachers "facilitators" instead of their deserved title of "teacher." Teachers should teach right from wrong, but since there is no right and wrong, the facilitators simply "introduce pupils to their options" and expose them to alternative ways of thinking and living, leaving the choices up to them. Math problems have become math exploration, so nobody has hurt feelings if they get the wrong answer. After all, any answer will do; it's not the end that counts, but the journey in getting there!

Anticulturalism

I believe this behavior is the fruit of a root called "anticulturalism." You may not even be aware of this term, coined by Kay Hymowitz, author of *Ready or Not*[7] and fellow at the Manhattan Institute, but it has touched your life to some degree. It is an erroneous trend rampant in the earth today, and it has permeated the minds of many believers.

- Anticulturalism implies that adults, attempting to mold the character of the young, are wrongfully using the power of the strong against the weak. In other words, children should develop independently, being allowed to go on their merry way, learning on their own what's best for them.

So even though the punks Junior picks to hang with look like they came from the county morgue, it's OK because "He's got to learn for himself who he is to become." And on Sundays he goes to church only "If he wants to, because he has to decide for himself what he believes about spiritual things." Susie eats, wears, listens to, and watches what she likes because "She has to make her own decisions about her life." This thinking subtly creeps into our psyche and can overrule our better judgment as kingdom parents.

---

[7] Hymowitz, Kay S. Ready or Not: What Happens When We Treat Children as Small Adults (San Francisco: Encounter Books, 2000).

• Anticulturalism is a tool of the devil to weaken our resolve as parents and render us powerless in our quest to train our children.

Parents only become impotent in childrearing when they *believe* they're powerless to impact their kids! So we live low and think, "Oh well, I'm not *really* happy with Junior or Susie's behavior, but it's pretty normal for a twelve-year-old. They have to learn for themselves. They'll figure it out. They're good kids." You continually lower the bar because, gosh, you don't want to be mean-spirited and demanding. They are kids, after all. This thinking is unbiblical

> **Anticulturalism is a tool of the devil to weaken our resolve as parents and render us powerless in our quest to train our children.**

nonsense and will hamstring us parents. Stop the music! Turn off the incessant drone of this world's tune. It's time to get serious with our kids.

As a parent I don't have it all, but the part I do have, I live out wholeheartedly, with great passion and deep conviction! I take courageous and bold steps forward in what I know. I don't move tentatively, displaying my insecurities and uncertainties. As the old saying goes, "Who wants to follow a general with an inferiority complex into battle?" Don't kid yourself; this is a battle, and *you must win!*

I think too many Christian parents today feel inferior in their parenting. We're afraid of what everybody thinks about us; we're afraid that our kids won't have friends; we're afraid that Susie and Junior won't be happy. But, *God hath not given us the spirit of fear* (2 Timothy 1:7). Fear is the opposite of faith, and if you allow it, your fleshly fears will cancel the promises God has given you. 1 Peter 3:14 says, *Do not fear what they fear; do not be frightened.*

Well, so and so thinks _____ is okay, so I guess I should let Susie _____ (*you fill in the blanks!*). Nonsense! You can't live to please aunties and grandmas and godparents and neighbors. You've got to stand up for what's right for you and your kids. This means that if your child is invited to a party, you simply ask, "Who's going to be there? Where are you going to be, Mom or Dad? Are movies planned for the occasion? Can we talk about some sensitive issues? I don't allow children to play in a room alone with the door shut. Any videos must be pre-approved by my husband or me before our boys can see them. These are some safeguards we've built into our lives, so please understand that it's not about your particular home or children, and it's not that I don't trust my boys." What I'm thinking, but may not say is: I don't trust the devil or the flesh, and I'm determined to preserve the innocence of my children by the grace of God! Ask questions. There are no bad questions when it comes to protecting your children.

> **Even when the family crew hovers on the edge of mutiny because we refuse to be moved from what the Holy Spirit has spoken, we parents must lead.**

Even when the family crew hovers on the edge of mutiny because we refuse to be moved from what the Holy Spirit has spoken, we parents must lead. I may be drowning in uncertainty, sensing weakness within, but I'm never willing to surrender my seat of authority. We must lead strongly, leaving no child wondering who's in charge.

It's time to sound the alarm, calling parents from their slumber and handing them back the reins of parenting. Mom and Dad, the world is assertively trying to peel your fingers off your kids so that you will hand them over to someone—anyone—else. But I'm here to say, "Refuse!" God wants to give you courage to rise up and lead your home. We don't get permission from the state, from our peers, or from our kids. We have permission from God to lead our homes, because as parents that is our number one priority after following the King.

CHAPTER SIXTEEN

Indulgence

Remind children that although they're extremely important, the earth still revolves around the sun.

—Fred G. Gosman

Another American disease which plagues many and particularly irks me is our obsession with making every activity fun for the kiddies. If it's not fun, kids won't want to do it, so "Let's make learning fun! Let's make work fun! Let's have fun at the dentist!" FUN, FUN, FUN! Fun is an *idol*. How unhealthy to set up such false expectations for our kids in every area of life!

True fun can only occur when it is the exception and not the rule. When my boys have too much fun for too long, their character suffers. They become selfish and sluggish, taking their blessings for granted and exuding a complaining spirit. We wonder why we have such poor service and workmanship at nearly every business we visit, from fast food restaurants and government agencies to department stores and gas stations, yet we continue to breed party animals. Throughout our world today, indulgence is ruining an entire generation.

To indulge means: yielding to the desire of, giving free rein to, catering to or humoring with special, excessive, or fond care. There's more! One who indulges becomes deeply involved with something subjectively felt as pleasant; they wallow, bask, luxuriate, revel, roll, rollick, and welter. Tell me, with a straight face, that this doesn't describe our culture.

Kids today know how to luxuriate, pamper, bask, and wallow in pleasure. They're massaged, bleached, waxed, and many get plastic surgery. They feed on Thai and sushi or guzzle gourmet coffee, while drinking in *Teen People*, *Cosmo Girl*, *GQ*, and *Seventeen* magazines. Cable TV is considered standard equipment. Since we don't have the guts to *impose our higher values* upon our sons and daughters, we find it easier to *indulge their lower natures*.

Junior has to be happy in the morning, so Fruit Loops or CoCo Puffs are fine, dear. Junior has to be happy with teacher, so Junior is *always right*. And he must be happy with homework, so Mommy will do it for him. If there's a problem with a playmate, Junior must be kept happy, which means *the other kid is always wrong*. Bedtimes must be happy too, so if you pitch a fit or shed a few manipulative tears, then you get to stay up with forty-year-old parents who have *earned* their bedtimes! Are *you* tired yet . . .? Just wait, there's more!

Happy kids must always be entertained, so "What programs do you have at church for little Susie?" Leisure time can't be dull, so let's buy something else to play with 'cause the show must go on! Happiness is always another snack, so stuff 'em full of fishy crackers, go-sugar-gogurts, fruitless roll-ups, and macaroni and cheese. Happy thirst must be quenched with a Coke and a smile, juiceless apple juice, and Frappucinos. When Mom and Dad need a break (is it any wonder?), the baby sitter (if they can find one who's willing!) must aim to please, so . . . house rules were made to be broken! If this kid lives at *your* house, you must be exhausted!

> Since we don't have the guts to *impose our higher values* upon our sons and daughters, we find it easier to *indulge their lower natures.*

Parents to the Rescue!

Bailing out our kids is so common today. They break it, we pick up the pieces. They lose it, we buy a new one. They blow it, we apologize and politic to cover their reputation, even to the point of defending their sin. How tragic! We work our tails off to enable them to live a lifestyle that is unreasonable, unaffordable, and harmful to their future homes and marriages.

Who will pick up the pieces, buy them a new one, politic for them, pay for their clothes, and fix their marriages five, ten, and twenty years from now? We say we want to raise giants in God. We say we want men and women who will stand up and preach and weep and sell out, but we are raising rock stars. "Oh darling, you need new clothes; let's hit the mall when I get off work." "Sure, you can play some more X-Box." "Oh baby, here's some cash for you to go see that new R-rated movie!" "Oh honey, just go and I'll clean it up for you." "I'll make your bed." "Oh sweetheart, I'll feed the dog." "You're too tired from football practice, you don't have to read the Word tonight." We are feeding a monster.

There is such passion in my soul to stop this insanity. Once again I've had opportunity to practice my conviction. Over the last year my ten-year-old has had to save and pay for four wristwatches because he's left them behind at the park, the beach, and other fun places he'd been playing. After each incident, we'd go back to where he last remembered having the watch, and we'd scour the area carefully, to no avail. He suggested he'd "be happy to go without" a watch since they had caused us all such stress and cost him so much money! But that wasn't an option since he's required to time his chores and reading and be on time for appointments. The watches cost fifteen dollars each, and since he doesn't have a regular job, it wasn't easy for him to pay. He even had to use his birthday money to reimburse me. But I knew I didn't have an option if I wanted to build into him a correct mind-set about what stuff costs.

If we pamper our children, they will act like royalty: arrogant, presumptuous, demanding, and unfit for any good work. If we don't parent them now, we will be parenting forever. One day, the husbands and wives of these indulged children will surely not deal so benevolently with their spouse if they are married to such a spoiled little boy or girl. To shield our children from all adversity, all unhappiness, all discomfort, and all discontent is to teach them incredible unreality and to build into them a foundation of me-first. They will not be prepared for the imminent reality of regular discomfort, discontent, and conflict with their future mate, boss, or roommate.

In this age of tolerance, when parents are not only tolerating, but encouraging such obscene decadence, I will not feel sorry for you when this monster of indulgence turns around to bite you. Remember, we deserve what we tolerate. Don't disqualify your kids from their incredible calling to leadership because you sinfully indulge them!

> **Remember, we deserve what we tolerate.**

Killing Our Kids with Kindness

One favorite reckless area of indulgence for many parents regards their child's eating habits. Now don't take me for a Scrooge. I am a party waiting to happen—just ask my boys! (As soon as they finish cleaning the house, mowing the yard, making dinner, building the shed, and feeding the poor, they'll tell you how much fun we have at our house—just kidding!) Sincerely, we have a blast together. Our house is Grand Central Station every single day, and we love to eat good food and lots of it! But for the sake of a good illustration that might jolt us into some reality about our culture's penchant for processed "food," indulge me—ha!—for a moment or two.

Envision the following scenario for a clearer illustration: It's a happy Saturday morning! Dad wakes early to the sound of birds singing and is filled with joy at the thought of one gloriously free day with no commitments whatsoever. No meetings, no games, no yard work, no garage sales to host, no relatives coming over, and no phone calls to make. Wow! He wakes Mom and proclaims it to be a day of adventure and fun for all!

After rolling groggy little ones out of bed, seeing them dressed with shoes tied, Dad announces it's a Krispy Kreme morning—as cheers and screams of delight abound. They pile into the car, heading for the big day. An hour later, when they can't poke one more donut down the hatch or slurp one more glass of ice cold milk, they make their way to the car. What delicious breakfast fun!

Now it's off to the local park where they play their hearts out on the jungle gym and work up a real appetite for some early lunch. Dad announces his intentions of treating all to some fine fare at Kentucky Fried Chicken. Soon they are sitting on benches, munching grease-laden fried chicken pieces, pasty instant potatoes, biscuits with margarine and sugar-filled jam, spoonfuls of corn drowned in fake butter, and baked beans slathered in syrupy sauce. And of course, let's not forget, they guzzle large soft drinks to wash it all down.

This indulged family heads off to an indoor Family Fun Center, where games are enjoyed by all, and tokens are earned to be spent on the immediate satisfaction of penny candies galore. As the afternoon winds down and all head home, Dad stops at Baskin Robbins for cones, and Mom picks up a couple of take-and-bake pizzas from the pizza kitchen next door. The day isn't over yet, and already this family has eaten truckloads of chemicals, sugars, artificial sweeteners, hydrogenated oils, trans fats, bleached flour, deep fried foods, and *absolutely not one ounce of nutrition.*

In treating our children we've often been tricked into harming them and setting them up for disaster, both short-term sugar malfunction and long-term health problems. Why is it that we often reward our kids in this toxic manner? We, and they, suffer the consequences of persistently administering this poison to them in body, soul, and spirit.

Perhaps it's time to reevaluate on a regular basis the *rewards* you're offering to your children rather than simply following the crowd to their favorite haunts when there's a reason to celebrate. Let's *not* become legalistic and entirely *un*realistic, but let's *do* determine to significantly shift our perspective and adjust our behavior if the treats we're offering our kids continually prove detrimental to their health and well-being.

Who's on the Almighty Throne?

If I was tempted to put anything in front of the King or the kingdom, it would be my kids. These boys are the absolute joy of my life. There is no place I'd rather be than at home with them. When our kids have such a huge part of our heart, we have to keep everything in balance. I'm obsessed with raising leaders, and I believe that our children are going to change the world, but they aren't gonna run my home in the meantime.

> **Kids are ruling so many homes today.**

Let's ask these questions:

- Do I feel I owe my children the good things in life while I take the leftovers?
- Must every weekend be a party for Junior, or he pouts?
- If one of my kids "gets blessed" do I feel I have to make it up to the others so it's even?
- Do I feel guilty asking my kids to spend the majority of their sunny Saturday working with me around the house, yard, or garage?
- Do my children dress more fashionably than me, at my expense?
- Do I feel badly when my kids have to sit in the back seat of the car when they'd much rather be up front?
- Is all my 'free time' driven by my kids' frivolous whims and preferred scheduling?

If we answered "yes" to any of the above questions, it's time to take the kid off the throne!

Kids are ruling so many homes today. Some of you are afraid of your own children. You want to please them. Forget about it! You cannot please a sinful little heart for more than half an hour or so! We must not seek to befriend our children at the cost of their inheritance in God. We weave in and out of friendship until they are about eighteen. Between now and then, we have to enlighten them to a lot of things they really don't want to know. It is a season of training, and much of the time, I'm the rod of correction! I've discovered that on many occasions, you must tell a child he is happy, even if

> **I've discovered that on many occasions, you must tell a child he is happy, even if he doesn't believe you!**

he doesn't believe you! Our home is not an oppressive place to live; don't hear that in what I'm saying. But biblical truth, not a whimsical child, has to rule our homes.

My kids and I have a lot of fun, but we can't be "best friends" during this season of their training. If you're afraid of your child now when he's four, what are you going to do when he's fifteen? He's going to run you out of the house! If you think I'm exaggerating, check out this news flash:

"Cat Barnard sits in her driveway in Enterprise, FL, Wednesday, December 8, 2004, next to the tent she and her husband Harlan slept in. The couple moved out of the house and set up the tent in the driveway going on strike because their children Benjamin, 17, and Kit, 12, refused to do household chores." (*Santa Fe Guide: Sunset Edition*, December 13, 2004)

This story is certainly a sign of the perilous times in which we're living. It reminds me of 2 Timothy 3:1–4 which warns: *But mark this: There will be terrible times in the last days. People will be lovers of themselves, lovers of money, boastful, proud, abusive, **disobedient to their parents**, ungrateful, unholy, without love, unforgiving, slanderous, without self-control, brutal, not lovers of the good, treacherous, rash, conceited, lovers of pleasure rather than lovers of God.*

Let's honestly face and label as the diabolical seeds they are, the tiny little indulgences we allow day after day toward our sons and daughters. These seeds which are being sown will ultimately destroy our children, our parental authority, our family relationships, and the culture around us.

Allowing Life's Difficulties to Touch My Boys

There is a quality and a substance of character that we long for our kids to have, but which can only be worked into their very fabric through difficulty. If we remove every trial and tribulation, every hard thing from their path, then there is nothing left for them to resist, oppose, or endure. We must love them enough to allow them to *struggle*. As a mom, I want every little thing to go smoothly, nicely, and easily. I want to rescue my boys from trials and shelter them from pain.

When I see others making choices that affect my boys negatively, I'm tempted to be critical of those people. I can plot an interception in my mind when I'm privy to an imminent correction, however gentle, that their dad or one of our church leaders is planning to bring to one of my sons. Or, when my answer won't bring my sons pleasure, sometimes I want to soft-soak it to dilute its strength.

I want to move things around to make the way easy for them. Everything within me wants the best for these little and big guys. But this is not love *in truth*. Sometimes their "best interest" means allowing them to experience life's hard knocks. Sometimes I want to be nicer than God.

We learn perseverance by pressing on, even though we don't get our own way. It's a natural fact of life for everyone. Children must be allowed to experience this most aggravating emotional experience. We don't always have to make things even-steven. Some days the scales will not balance no matter how hard you try. This is simply reality. Life is not equitable in all circumstances. We must stop trying to be the "almighty balancer of the scales" for our children if we're going to see our kids become the kind of leaders God can use.

The kind of leaders we raise up in our homes and in our local churches will determine how effective we are and how long we remain effective. How do we expect to produce strong leaders if we don't allow strength to be built through trial? Muscle is built by resistance. Patience is produced by painful endurance. Character is cultivated when circumstances bring disappointment.

Friends, think for a moment. When have we learned our most valuable lessons and experienced our finest moments along the path of life? My answer has to be: during trial, hardship, and contrary circumstances. It was truly while traveling along the roads of perseverance and endurance that my leadership capacity was enlarged the most.

Why then do we long to shield our children from difficulties and rob them of the blessing of true character riches? How will our children remain committed through thick and thin in marriage if they were never required to endure hardships along the way? What kind of parents will they be, having never grown up themselves?

> **It was truly while traveling along the roads of perseverance and endurance that my leadership capacity was enlarged the most.**

This spiritual and character development through pain and perseverance is well illustrated in the Mira men's power-lifting pastime. Several days a week you'll find our sons in the garage pumping iron with their daddy. It is an environment chock-full of resistance. The noises they make indicate severe struggle, even pain. But their vision keeps them pressing on in the process of building hard-earned muscle which they know can come no other way.

This passage seems fitting. Perhaps you could tack it up on the wall for you and the kids to memorize: *Consider it pure joy, my brothers, whenever you face trials of many kinds, because you know that the testing of your faith develops perseverance. Perseverance must finish its work so that you may be mature and complete, **not lacking anything** (James 1:2–4).*

CHAPTER SEVENTEEN

Weeding the Garden

I think it is in our interest to punish the first insult because an insult unpunished is the parent of many others.
—Thomas Jefferson 1785

People ask me if I garden and I answer, "The only garden I have time for is the one where I'm growing my five kids. They're full of weeds." It's up to us to garden our children's lives in such a way that they flourish like a productive field. They should yield abundant fruit and ample provision to share with the masses, thus becoming a blessing to nations! What are we doing with this fertile soil, teeming with the richness of God's natural resource? How do we cultivate and work this rich land of our children's lives, thus realizing the possibility residing within them?

I don't know about you, but at our house we've got to continually hoe, fertilize, and prune our living plants, pulling those training bands snug against the standard God has given us. The attention it takes to nurture them is all-consuming. Their neglect is unforgiving. That little seed of stubbornness you ignore today will grow and multiply if left long enough. The end result will be an unmanageable teenager who had his way as a preschooler and was left unrestrained.

This reminds me of a blackberry vine, common to our region. Seemingly innocent and laden with tiny blossoms and luscious fruit, it cunningly begins to work its way into and around anything within its proximity. Before long, our city government is found spending loads of taxpayer money to destroy these prolific, thorn-covered, resistant, weed ropes which have become intolerable nuisances to our homes, yards, streets, and parks. No matter how cute and sweet they once were, they've become a nightmare! Children in their growing-up years have the same potential if left to themselves. How much public money is spent in our cities nationwide to manage the sins of our youth?

Weeding in our homes may be left undone because it's hard, unpleasant work, and weeds are persistent. Often times, parents have allowed such a crop to grow that they don't want their kids anywhere near them. Just being in the same room with an "uncultivated" child gives the same painful sensation as that of blackberry thorns digging into our skin. I know because at times those sneaky weeds have worked their way into my child's character until I've had to declare out-and-out war! This human gardening requires exhaustive patience and face-to-face interaction if we're going to see valuable character qualities blossom.

When I look upon the condition of multitudes of adults today, I grieve over the harmful character flaws which have overtaken these gardens: laziness, self-indulgence, moodiness, self-centeredness, stinginess, addictions, disorganization, unhealthy eating patterns, and more. Each of these vices has a root that could have been dealt with so many years ago.

When children are young and easily trainable like tender shoots, it is easy to stake those vines and adjust their growth pattern. But we ignore it, saying "They're just kids," "Boys will be boys," or "It's child's play." We fail to see it as a snare, a deadly pattern which we are encouraging and actually training into our young plantings. Proverbs 19:18 urges us to *discipline your son, for in that there is hope; do not be a willing party to his death.* How detrimental these flaws will become to our children if left to flourish! If only we could see the end result from our patterns of parenting, rather than live for the moment. What cruel hatred to accommodate sin in our children!

> **How much public money is spent in our cities nationwide to manage the sins of our youth?**

Put the Axe to the Root

Sooner or later, weeds always come to the surface, souring our kid's countenance. You've likely seen "the look" show up at your house. You know "the look," the defiant expressions of rebellion, gloom, childish disappointment, contempt, boredom, or aloofness toward elders. There is no excuse for your son or daughter to have that look on their face if you don't like it. Let's break out of normal and change the look on that face. Let's use the tools God has given us for leverage to take hold of our homes and clearly lead.

If you don't like the effects of the skateboard, lock it up until the attitude changes. If that hat seems to bring an air of punk to your leader-in-the-making, confiscate the hat.

We have to put the axe to the root of these pesky weeds and take decisive measures. There's a stick in my house, and the kids know that when I reach for the stick, the party's over. The bigger they get, the bigger the stick. Sticks turn into yanked car keys, loss of electronics' privileges, and a moratorium on social engagements.

You better be ruthless with those weeds because baby weeds turn into giant, resistant vines. If you're going to nurture that prickly little shoot, it's going to turn around and put a stranglehold on the life in your home. If God is bringing things to your mind even now, write them down. You are not thinking higher than God. God's just trying to raise your standard. For your kid's sake, He's trying to tell you to make necessary adjustments.

You can't play schoolmates with your children. Be the parent that your child needs and the adult God expects you to be. Remember that your goal is not a happy child, but one of character and substance. Whether they like it or not, you are the boss. You can be the boss without being bossy or defensive. Lines of authority can be drawn without acting ugly or pushing your weight around. If you are in control, you needn't be loud or overbearing. You can calmly, and with a smile on your face, sentence your child to solitary confinement.

Weed Feed

Most youngsters across the globe wholeheartedly enjoy playing their (or their friends') video games: X-Box, Playstation 2, or GameCube. Without ever reading a manual, their passion and expertise for "staying alive" boggles the mind. I imagine they could play for hours, perhaps days, without eating, drinking, or taking a bathroom break because these little devils (the games, not the kids!) are so engaging.

If your child is spending inordinate amounts of time engaged in these devices, I'd like to stir you from your indifference into actively limiting these amusements. Such seemingly innocuous, amoral gaming systems could be threatening to dwarf the leadership capacity of your child.

By allowing this indulgence, parents inadvertently teach their kids to "check out" of family life. They become selfish, passive, mentally turned-off, and physically weakened from their lack of bodily exertion. Some folks figure, "Well, if Junior wants to play X-Box all day, no problem. At least he's out of my hair." But what's convenient and peaceful for us isn't always the best thing for our kids in the long run. One day my nine-year old said to me, "Momma, you know how much I like X-Box, but it's addictive. You know I could really be addicted to it if I let myself."

> **Lines of authority can be drawn without acting ugly or pushing your weight around.**

Mom and Dad, I beg you not to indulge your child's electronic appetite! Don't be party to this crime of dumbing down your kids when their time could be spent becoming great through serving others, reading good books, helping around the house, and keeping younger siblings contented. On occasion, if a privilege has been earned and consistent godly character is displayed, I'll allow our boys to enjoy an afternoon of gaming in our rec room. In our rainy climate here in the Seattle area, it would be easy to be lenient with these devices. We've been given four different varieties of these mechanical contraptions. Thankfully, they mostly sit very alone in their boxes.

Unplug your kids! *Require* them to enjoy the outdoors for hours of creative fun and frolic in the yard, at the park, on their bikes, or walking that dog they begged you to get for them! Take back your authority in this electronic arena if things are out of hand with videos, games, computers, and internet use. Take a stand against the domination of these machines in the life of your youngsters.

Weeding Junior's Diet

Our children need to be guided in their diet. Some parents ought to be arrested because of how they're feeding their children! Everywhere I go, kids seem to be existing on carbs: chips, white bread, crackers, white rice, and other non-nutritive, refined products. There is so much bargaining going on: a truce here, a compromise there. "A little grumpy?" Let's make it all better with some chocolate!

Have you met, "the picky kid?" He may be living in your house! I'm continually grieved and not a little irritated by the hordes of picky eaters who visit our home. I bumped into one at a barbecue recently, and we had this uncomfortable interlude: "Can I have more chips?" he begged, as the lonely grilled burger, ice-cold watermelon, and pasta salad with fresh veggies sat waiting patiently on his paper plate at this particular picnic. "Can I? Can I?" I poured a drink into his cup, ignoring his pleas for more chips. "Is that pop? I want pop! Is that pop?" "No, it's water," I finally answered. "We don't have pop." His face fell to his knees, and he never did eat the food on his plate.

Little ones are being trained to eat only what makes their mouths happy. Our taste buds are a blank slate at birth. We *acquire* tastes by *practice*. In Mexico, children learn to love beans, rice, salsa, and corn tortillas. In India, no child grows up without their share of curry. In Africa the children thrill at Bovril, a spread on toast that would make most Americans gag! These are foods administered to the local children from infancy. They've become accustomed to the spices and vibrant flavors over time. Because taste buds adjust to what hits them, we need to insist that our kids eat food which is whole, real, and nutritive.

"My Kid Won't Eat Healthy Food!"

Have you noticed all the journalistic space dedicated to the "dilemma" of getting little Junior to eat his veggies? I can't quite relate to a crisis of this magnitude, especially pertaining to a forty-pound child. My five boys have always been expected to eat what's set before them according to Luke 10:8: *When you enter a town and are welcomed, eat what is set before you.* But in today's touchy-feely, politically-correct culture, sometimes common sense gets thrown right out the window. Parents find themselves confused about very simple matters. So, what to do about your picky eater? Let's be discerning in an age of preschooler-pleasing parents.

1. Try taking the candy (processed sugar and white flour, a.k.a., refined carbs) out of Junior's left hand. I never cease to be amazed by moms who overlook what their little ones are consuming throughout the day, so when meal times roll around, there is no hunger to motivate them to eat something healthful. Pizza, chicken fingers, and noodles are what little boys and girls seem to be made of these days, but there's about zilch in the nutrition factor of these tempting little taste treats. Clean out the cupboards and refrigerator and cut out in-between meal munching, unless you're offering fresh fruit, sliced veggies, and natural peanut butter and honey on whole grain toast. You'll be amazed at what a hungry kid will eat!

2. Try the "eat it or go hungry" line. Mean it. Enforce it. Buddy Hackett said, "My mother's menu consisted of two choices: Take it or leave it." Don't wimp out and fix two meals. You're not a short-order cook. You're a hard-working parent who happens to be training up those little ones to live healthy and grateful lives. Don't limit your kid's future by training him to eat only what he likes. Train him to learn to like new stuff. It really will work!

3. Last resort, eat or suffer. Yes, on the rare occasion when absolutely necessary, I have spanked a kid and then made him eat the cause of the violation.

Side note: This morning, slow-cooked oatmeal was served for the fifth day in a row for breakfast at our house. I told the boys that we'll be having oatmeal each morning until I see a very happy heart when their eyes hit the breakfast table. Not only is oatmeal hugely nutritious, building our bodies and cleansing our systems, it is a tasty, filling dish, especially with dried fruit, a little honey, and organic butter and milk on top.

Spoiled American children regularly turn their noses up at healthful foods. We should be ashamed of ourselves if we let them get away with it.

CHAPTER EIGHTEEN

Veneer Is Not Enough

If honor be your clothing, the suit will last a lifetime; but if clothing be your honor, it will soon be worn threadbare.

—William Arnot

Make every effort to add to your faith goodness; and to goodness, knowledge; and to knowledge, self-control; and to self-control, perseverance; and to perseverance, godliness; and to godliness, brotherly kindness; and to brotherly kindness, love.

—1 Peter 1:5–7

Why does it seem like so few of our youth have any substance to them? Shallow is how I sum up the masses I meet here and there all over America and across the globe. I'm not saying they're stupid, incapable, or uneducated. By far, they are the most "educated" of all generations. But their huge, God-given potential remains largely untapped. They are skating on the surface of life. The veneer of their person, that thin ornamental coating giving them a superior appearance, is only a superficial layer covering an inferior reality. This under-developed generation seems to be motivated only by what they can touch, taste, see, smell, or hear. They are propelled by pleasure at every level. Parents and educational systems have not only allowed this condition, but encouraged it. "How?" you might ask.

Consider the mom or dad who is overly impressed with our sophisticated sports culture, high academic achievement, or the importance of social status. Their focus on these extremely flimsy surface issues is interpreted by their kids as *paramount*. It becomes the goal, the focus, and the unhealthy measure of value for that young man or woman. These temporal, unbiblical values then take precedence over the substantial and eternally lasting issues of life.

The importance of a daily prayer life, study of God's Word, godly character development, strong convictions, and an active kingdom-building and evangelistic lifestyle are what *ought* to reign supreme. When Mom's concern is over hair, dress, make-up, figure, and Susie's need for friends, then Susie's life will be built upon the sands of these fleeting and fickle surface issues. Her time, talk, and thoughts will center on these relatively unimportant matters. Chasing after brand names, popularity, possessions, "freedom," independence, sleek vehicles and social status is all such a huge waste of time. Encouraging such temporal frivolities will prove to be a poison injected into the very fiber of our children's being.

> **Parents, we must go deeper.**

Parents, we must go deeper. For one, let's lead our kids by keeping our own hearts clean, teaching them to do the same. This verse from Proverbs reminds us that what's inside is going to come out sooner or later, affecting every area of our lives. *Keep your heart with all diligence, for out of it spring the issues of life* (Proverbs 4:23, NKJV).

We cannot harbor enemies within. Anger, jealousy, lust, hurt, and offense are poison to our lives. We cannot embrace such enemies of our souls who constantly vie for a foothold. We must pray that God puts a wall of protection around our hearts! We must ruthlessly make war upon the first hint of these enemies at our gates! I must teach my children that bitterness is a deadly poison. Ron McManus puts it this way: "Bitterness is like drinking poison and waiting for the other person to die." Let's teach our sons and daughters to stand watch at the door of their hearts.

Sulking

We've also got to train our kids to guard their outward expressions, even when all is not well with their soul! If we allow our children to sulk and pout when they aren't happy with our decisions, we encourage unhealthy stuff to fester inside of them. Tell them that bad moods are not allowed in your home, so they'll go back to bed if they're grumpy and get back up on the right side of the bed. It's a matter of their will. They *can* control their moods. Their emotions cannot be allowed to sit on the throne.

When we spank them, they may cry softly into their pillows—no tantrums, shrieking, fits of rage, and rebellion. If they are curt after a wise and properly measured spanking, they will receive another until there is humility, submission, and repentance. Never subtly apologize for punishing: "Daddy loves you, *but* I will not let you rebel." Instead, firmly reassure, "Daddy loves you *so much* that he refuses to allow you to rebel."

Self-Control

Often, my voice can be heard exhorting any one of my sons, "*Self-control*, my boy!" Without self-control, our sons and daughters will be like cities with broken-down walls: open to the enemy and other evil predators (Proverbs 25:28). Walls were *key* to cities being protected in Bible times. A city without walls didn't have a hope of surviving! *A child lacking self-control is left vulnerable to enemies within and without.*

I have one particular child, who will remain anonymous, who has a particularly difficult time with this principle of self-restraint, due, I think, to his extremely animated personality. However, personality and gifting must be guarded and guided by our better judgment. His brother turned to him one day and said, "Spiritual seat belts are what you need. The problem is you're driving the car, and you need to put on your restraining device." It's a great illustration of what we're speaking of here. Our children must drive the car of their lives, always wearing their seat belt of self-control in order to get them safely to their destination.

It's so tempting for boys to be physically aggressive when they're angry or want their own way. "Getting physical," as we say in our home, stirs up intense anger and puts walls between brothers. We can't wink at these incidents when they occur in our homes between siblings. We must match the punishment to the offense. Violence in a home is unacceptable.

I'm not referring to "wrestling," one of my husband's favorite games to play with his boys. The kids love it! When they start to roll, I get outta' the way. Having all boys, they engage with all their might, faces red, elbows flying, tying each other in knots and bending themselves like rubber bands. At times it gets a bit rough—all in fun—and my boys have urged me not to worry. "It's a guy thing," they assure me. Being a woman, I'm more comfortable with baking cookies or playing card games together calmly, but guys gotta rumble! There are healthy ways for boys to get physical, and we have to discern the difference.

It's our responsibility to help develop their "self-control muscle" so that it naturally responds when provoked. Galatians 5:22 says self-control is a fruit of the Holy Spirit, and it should be obvious in our kids' lives. They'll be equipped for life with this powerful weapon of self-control in their arsenal. Such a tool should be at the ready, so they don't lash out as a mere man would.

> **They'll be equipped for life with this powerful weapon of self-control in their arsenal.**

Rude Interruptions

Picture this: Two adults are engaged in conversation when suddenly a little tyke runs up, exploding with questions, demands, and other "urgent" matters, and completely disrupts the discussion between the adults. Who gave this three-foot-high little guy the power to derail the progressive communication between these two 150-pound adults, three times his size? Why does this child suddenly become the main attraction, taking center stage when no blood is running, a fire isn't threatening, and a terrorist has not entered the building? Easy. His mother and father haven't trained him to handle himself with restraint.

Instead, his parents have *trained* him that at the drop of a hat, he may have his way, rudely barging in where his nose doesn't belong. Stop this self-centered behavior. Train him or her to walk up quietly and gently place his or her hand on your arm or side, never saying a word or making a peep; the child then waits for you to decide when it is appropriate for him to speak, not the other way around. This is big stuff that may seem like small stuff, but big doors swing on small hinges. This seemingly tiny hinge of self-control will serve your child hugely in more ways than you can imagine.

Government Is Not a Bad Word

Along the same line, if our children don't learn to govern themselves, they will have to be governed by others all their lives. *Government* is the exercise of authority over a particular sphere. *Self* refers to one's own person as distinct from all others. Put these two together and there you have it: *self-government*. Self-government is something we need to work into our kids' understanding and conduct.

Sadly, self-government is a rarity among the masses. More often than not, society exhibits mob-rule rather than self-rule. Pervasive troubles are brewing due to the lack of this aspect of character development. If our children can't govern themselves all alone when no one else is looking, they haven't mastered this muscle.

Institutions like jails, prisons, detention centers, reform schools, and juvenile halls are designed for those sons and daughters who have not learned to self-govern. Such deviants find themselves in one very long "time-out" because they didn't master their own passions and desires. If I have to be present to get my kids to do the right thing, then they haven't

> Institutions like jails, prisons, detention centers, reform schools, and juvenile halls are designed for those sons and daughters who have not learned to self-govern.

120

developed the art of self-government. If character is "what we are when no one else is watching," how do your kids rate? Be ruthless on this one.

"Oh, She's Shy"

Many young children I meet will not look me in the eye. Their parents stand there pleading with them to greet me, and they refuse. They drop their faces and contort their bodies. They'll even turn and kick a sibling or fight over a toy as I'm standing there waiting, but they won't respond to me. I am amazed. "She's shy," Dad says with a nervous laugh. But she's not shy when dessert is served or she's handed a gift. First impressions are hard to erase. There is no excuse for such unacceptable behavior.

Shy is a lie. Children shouldn't be allowed to be shy, and greetings should not be optional. Let me add: they ought to be warm and cheerful, with eye contact and an outdoor speaking voice. Responding to adult situations is imperative, even for the two-year-old among us. First impressions can be a weapon in God's hand. Teach your children to shake hands firmly while they look the new acquaintance in the eye. Putting our best foot forward is imperative in God's economy. That's what leaders should do. Every child is to be a leader according to 1 Timothy 4:12: *Don't let anyone look down on you because you are young, but set an example for the believers in speech, in life, in love, in faith and in purity.*

> **First impressions can be a weapon in God's hand.**

If you've trained your children to acknowledge adults in some particular manner, their refusal to do so is rebellion to your authority. Don't ignore it. One day I lined up my sons and spanked them for not shaking hands with a gentleman I had introduced them to earlier in the day. Their improper response showed a lack of respect and honor toward the man.

"Shyness" takes on many forms. We've got to be discerning in these matters in order to parent effectively. My youngest son was in a school performance and his group of four and five-year olds were preparing to sing. I had observed a pattern in his life I knew I had to adjust, so I gave my son a firm, but loving, exhortation. I told him he was not to look down at the ground during his performance. This expression of pretending to be shy would not be allowed because he isn't shy. Even if he tended to be shy, I wouldn't indulge him in the habit because I don't think it's a helpful pattern according to 2 Timothy 1:7: *For God did not give us a spirit of timidity, but a spirit of power, of love and of self-discipline.*

I understand God creates diverse personalities, but each of them, whether quiet and gentle or charismatic and demonstrative, should be bold in humility, chin up, in Christ's strength. I said, "You are strong and courageous and bold, and you're a leader, so get up there and keep your chin up." After the program, I noted with enthusiasm that he had kept his chin up and participated well. He said, "Mommy, my face wanted to be shy but I said no." That's what self-control is: When our hands want to do something wrong, we tell our hands "no," or if our leg wants to kick someone, we tell our leg "no!"

Remind your child that self-control is a fruit of the Holy Spirit. Don't underestimate the power of God as this fruit is expressed in your youngster! Teach him to call upon God and to expect God's *grace to help in time of need* (Hebrews 4:16, KJV).

Take your place in your child's life, and wrest from within him or her that dynamic divine treasure. When we work in partnership with an awesome God, we can expect greatness to rise up on every occasion needed in the lives of our boys and girls.

CHAPTER NINETEEN

For the Glory of God!

Declare his glory among the nations, his marvelous deeds among all peoples. **For great is the LORD and most worthy of praise;** *he is to be feared above all gods . . . Ascribe to the LORD, O families of nations,* **ascribe to the LORD glory and strength.**
— Psalms 96:3–7

I can still hear the faint voices of those who said, "You are so idealistic, Denise. A dreamer. Give it up. Come talk to me in twenty years when reality has hit you." Here I sit, twenty-five years later, never once disappointed by holding up the idealistic truth of Scripture and never once failed by the One who wrote the Book. Mere humans tried to prophesy my failure and quench my fire, but I must tell you, *God is not a man that He should lie,* according to Numbers 23:19. Similarly, Romans 3:4 exhorts us to *let God be true and every man a liar.* Stand on the Rock, and you will not be put to shame.

Isaiah 61:9 promises us, *"Their descendants will be known among the nations, and their offspring among the peoples. All who see them will acknowledge that they are a people the LORD has blessed."* People will see our kids, and they will say, "These are a people the Lord has blessed," not "they are the perfect parents." All the glory goes to God. It's not about, "Oh, how well Denise and Gregory have done this parenting thing!" But rather, "Oh, how awesome it is that God will come and rest on human flesh and do amazing things!" It's not, "They did it all right or are doing it all right," *A thousand times no!* The reality is "Oh, how big our God is if we will dare to believe Him to work through our frail human flesh!"

That understanding removes from us such pressure to perform! So many parenting books are a checklist of righteous acts, but if we rest on our own strength, our own ideas of right and wrong, we will bring legalism into our homes. We will lose our kids. We will produce cynical, tired, rebellious offspring. We must be Spirit-led and not led by our best moral law and society's standards.

I cannot take credit—this confession is so freeing! It doesn't rest on me to produce godliness in my sons. What relief! I sit back and see the glory of God, *not* the glory of men. It is to His glory for what He has done. I couldn't produce my sons' particular strengths, giftings, and capabilities. These things did not come from me. If this was something I could do, then I would tell you how good I am. But this is not something I can do.

This is where we lean on Him and say, "It is Jesus!" I know in my flesh dwells no good thing. I know that I live right where you live, behind the same front doors, behind the same mini-blinds, facing similar challenges and slaying common giants. I know my weaknesses. I know we are just conduits through which God's Spirit can work. Picture water flowing through a section of very disposable PVC pipe. That's how I see it as God speaks through my husband and me and uses us to do His work in our home. We are simply channels of His grace and power used to accomplish His purposes. If you lived in my house, you'd know that anything precious that comes to pass in our children comes from Him.

The Grace of God in Parenting

There are moments when I have to catch my breath because I am so stunned at the marvelous, unmerited grace of God in my sons. The reality of God's grace overwhelms me as I survey the passing years, the sweet fruit in my children's lives, and the painful days of lack when I had so seemingly little to offer them. God met me in my famine and fed me

> I am persuaded that childrearing is impossible for me without the greatness of my God.

bread from heaven. I am persuaded that childrearing is impossible for me without the greatness of my God. I am convinced that my efforts are worthless, and at best I am striving without the grace of God.

I've never been a well-oiled machine when it came to mothering, parenting, and discipling my children. I felt more like a tire with a constant leak. It seemed to me that I was always working from a deficit, feeling like I wasn't measuring up, and so painfully aware of my weaknesses. All my limitations, my inabilities, and my perceived dearth of resources, both human and financial, seemed glaring to me when it came to bringing up baby. But God . . . . "This is my story, this is my song, praising my Savior all the day long!" I would be robbing God if I took credit for the evidences of His kingdom that I see in my kids. Their lives shout aloud the abundant outpouring of the grace of God. Any gold you find in them has come from Him.

My part in the matter is prayer, prayer, and more prayer. My anguished pleas for help have not gone unanswered. My often lonely journey through the years has been met by my best friend, Jesus. I would find myself time and again, on my knees, bankrupt for answers, wrestling for what seemed my very next breath. Never did He leave me. Never did He leave my sons.

I would look around and it seemed like others parented so naturally and with ease. Not me. I rarely found it easy. I don't mean my sons were difficult. *I* was difficult. I was not naturally gifted to be what I felt I needed to be for them. They were so gifted, so obviously brilliant and creative. *I* was the problem. My fears and insecurities, my nagging sense of failure, my organizational challenges, and my temptation to allow emotions to rule me have been some of my handicaps. I often struggled to find my way through. Seeing how God has transcended my particular weaknesses with His power, assures me that any parent postured toward Him will find success as they embark on this journey of parenting.

I love my sons deeply, but know that in myself I am weak and ignorant regarding raising leaders in my home. By His grace and out of pure necessity, more often than not I lean on Jesus Christ. I cannot even take credit for this thread of genius—depending on Him—woven throughout our family's history. For indeed, out of my wrecked nature, I have found the secret to parenting—trust wholly in our Savior and King!

> . . . out of my wrecked nature, I have found the secret to parenting— trust wholly in our Savior and King!

The ABCs of Practical Parenting

Attitude

A happy heart, eyes, mouth, shoulders, and feet are expected at our house. Even voice tones denote submission to authority or a lack thereof. None of that "standing-up-on-the-outside while sitting-down-on-the-inside" stuff. What must be done must be done with a happy heart, otherwise known as a "good attitude." A sinful attitude in our home is as much a violation as a sinful act. Psalms 51:10 is a prayer we can teach our children: *Create in me a clean heart, O God; and renew a right spirit within me* (KJV).

Attitude is a tiny thing that makes a world of difference. Remember, giant doors swing on small hinges. Continually oil this hinge of attitude in your children, not allowing it to creak and groan and moan and huff and puff.

Bedrooms with My View

Where your children sleep is not their exclusive and private domain with inherent rights and privileges. Most of the time, the Mira kids have had to share a room with one or more siblings. It's been good for them. It has also strategically placed spies in the right place at the right time. I'm laughing as I write this, because I'm determined not to allow any of our boys to enjoy the title of favored tattletale. But I must say, there is safety in numbers!

If your kid's room is shrouded in mystery, then get in there with him or her and do a "spring" cleaning, even if it's snowing outside! Team together, and dig into every nook and cranny. Cleanse it of any unacceptable magazines, posters (nothing sensual or scary allowed), games, books, decor, and inappropriate clothing. I'm careful to knock on doors of adolescents before I turn the handle. I respect the fact that their developing bodies—along with training bras and athletic support gear—are sources of extreme modesty. But I don't cower from stepping boldly through the door to greet them and have a (casual☺) look around once I get the OK. Our children should have nothing hidden in their rooms of which they would be ashamed, as should be true of us, their parents.

Bored Kids

At our house, bored kids will meet with hard work. If they even hint at the "B" word, Mom whips out the extra chore list faster than a speeding bullet. There are always cars to wash, gardens to weed, porches to sweep, and garages to clean. With a closet full of games, good books to read, art supplies, musical instruments, Legos, and action figures, there is no excuse to be bored. Don't forget they also have a kitchen equipped to cook up a storm and a free country with wide open spaces in which to run. There's something fun for everyone. I think "bored" is a mind-set of spoiled little boys and girls. It's also a maneuver to get Mom and Dad to rent another movie to watch. Don't fall for it!

Busy, Busy, Busy . . .

I think our busyness lends to indulging our children. Because our priorities are wrong, our schedules become chaotic. Since we're not where we should be, ruling our sphere and engaging with our kids, we don't want to fight when we finally do get home where we belong. Far too often we don't want to sour the family atmosphere with conflict over anything, so we indulge, indulge, indulge to keep the peace with our kids. In actuality, we're reinforcing wrong behavior, propping up a sense of elation that is a lie, and feeding cat's meat to a crocodile. Chaos complicates! Just by streamlining our lives and simplifying our schedules we'll find it easier to parent effectively.

Chore Charts

Chore charts have changed our lives. Funny what excites us once we're parents, huh? Begin your day and your child's day with a plan, and there will be peace. Kids want a goal and need to know what's expected of them, rather than always being randomly yanked from their play throughout the day to do one spontaneous chore after another at a parent's disorganized whim. Of course we can do it that way because we are the authority in the home, but it's not the optimum method.

Life happens, and sometimes that's how it goes. However, I don't want to exasperate my kids on a daily basis due to my lack of planning ahead. Simply make a list of what needs to be done throughout the week to keep your home livable according to your (reasonable) standards. Estimate the time each of these chores will take. Divvy them up between the siblings, taking into consideration their ages, capabilities, etc. Don't be too hard on the oldest or too easy on the youngest.

I then produce a basic chart under the "table" option on Microsoft Word, but you can do it with a ruler and a pen if need be. The chart is not in charge, as other things do come up along the way, but it's a great tool to have in place on most days. This is definitely a working document! Our charts change as needs change (watering the garden happens in summer, shoveling snow in winter), but not weekly or even monthly. Here are two examples of our chore charts. The first is for ages seven to eight, and the second is for ages twelve to thirteen. Grey boxes indicate which day of the week the listed chore is required to be done. The numbers inside the grey boxes are approximations of time needed to complete the task listed.

Week:	SETH DANIEL					Age 7–8	
Responsibility	MON	TUE	WED	THU	FRI	SAT	SUN
Bible reading/journal							
Bed made/room tidy B4 breakfast							
Teeth brushed/floss/ slippers on B4 school							
Unload/load dishes a.m.							
Clean downstairs bathroom	15				Floor 20		
9 Trash collected/new liners if needed	7			7			
Check and refill 5 soap dispensers		10					
Recycle to outside bins		8				8	
Count 4 rolls toilet paper in 4 bathrooms					7		
Vacuum steps/(Sweep tile Friday)			Vac 10		Sweep 7		

Deliver all linens/towels/ put away your clothes	▓	▓	▓	▓	▓	▓	
Mailbox job	▓	▓	▓	▓	▓	▓	
Shower nightly unless excused	▓	▓	▓	▓	▓	▓	▓
Clothes laid out for church						▓	
Read daily 45 minutes	▓	▓	▓	▓	▓		
Keep house tidy-pick up your stuff	▓	▓	▓	▓	▓	▓	▓

Week:	LEVI						Age 12–13
Responsibility	MON	TUE	WED	THU	FRI	SAT	SUN
Bed made, room tidy, drawers clean, hair styled B4 breakfast	20	20	20	20	20		20
Breakfast eaten/brush teeth & FLOSS	20	20	20	20	20		20
Bible/journal begins after brushing teeth	▓	▓	▓	▓	▓	▓	
Dishwasher unload/load as needed	▓	▓	▓	▓	▓	▓	
Piano practice 40 minutes	▓	▓	lesson	▓	▓	▓	
DAILY DUTIES- Get mail-Check water bottle-Trash out- Fill pellet stove AS NEEDED!!!	▓	▓	▓	▓	▓	▓	

Vacuum and mop ALL downstairs Pergo (bath too)/scrub sink, scrub counters/stove top	15						
Vacuum and mop all wood/ Pergo main level—NOT bath—<u>On and Under kitchen rugs too.</u>				30			
Empty all trash cans (3 downstairs, 1 main, 1 upstairs, laundry room mini-bin) replace liners if needed				7			
Boys' bathroom: Fresh towel placed on rack both days! Thursday-hand scrub behind toilet and around border of bathroom		10 toilet/ Sink /mirror			20 +Floor Shower tub		
Vacuum Downstairs & Upstairs (empty filters regularly) and Master Bedroom-big vac 1st Wed			25				
Levi delivers kids & parents clothes/put away clothes	5	5	5	5	5		
Clothes for TOMORROW laid out							

Computers with Internet Access in Bedrooms

Personal computers with internet access in your kid's bedroom with the door shut? Why not just host a private party for the devil? Let's not naively think our children are above falling prey to the seductive e-mails, chat rooms, and other schemes of the enemy of their souls. Pop-ups alone can qualify as pornography! Friends, let's face it, even the manner in which news is reported has become like an R-rated scandal sheet. A life of hermitage in the bedroom with the door shut isn't good enough for your extraordinary child! Unplug Junior and read him a good book!

Devo(yawn)tions

A well-known Christian psychologist and author was vulnerably sharing how he used to set up an overhead projector at home to do lengthy Bible studies with his young children. He stopped when he realized he was on the devil's side! His academic approach was turning his boys off to God. I've been there and done that, too. Not with a projector, but in my own heavy-handed way.

In every form and fashion, I have attempted to get the Word into my kids. (See God's Word, pp. 134–135.) Some methods have been seamless and anointed; while others have been very dry. We can be confident that whether our Bible and prayer times have been "heavenly," or "not-so-heavenly," they are never wasted according to Isaiah 55:11 in which God says, *My Word that goes out from my mouth . . . will not return to me empty, but will accomplish what I desire and achieve the purpose for which I sent it.*

I think the best way to equip our families spiritually is God's way. His naturally supernatural way makes the Word of God and prayer a way of life. Be consistent, but don't try so hard that it becomes mechanical and binding, bringing death instead of life.

Model a lifestyle of living in the Word and loving God above all else. Realize there are seasons in life. Every season brings change. The methods that have worked for me are many and varied and have been practiced in the appropriate season. They include:

1. Bible time around the breakfast table with Mom reading Proverbs aloud from *The Living Bible* and inviting input and practical application from two, three, and four-year olds.
2. Bible time using the *One-Year Bible for Kids* or the adult *One-Year Bible*, keeping sticker charts and celebrating the year's grand achievement with a dinner party and special friends.
3. Bible time reading mountains of colorful and exciting Bible stories for children. Day after day after day of cozy time, snuggling with Mommy or Daddy before naptime, bedtime, or anytime.
4. Private Bible time one-on-one with Mom when one child just seemed to be in a season when he needed more personal direction and attention.

Find what fits your brood, your mood, and your season. Formal Bible studies with accompanying manuals weren't my style, but they may be yours. Morning or after lunch have been our chunky Bible reading times, but you might be nocturnal. The vital ingredient is consistency. Remember, young leaders cannot survive on bread alone, but on every Word that comes from the mouth of God (Paraphrase, Matthew 4:4).

Over the years our boys also enjoyed lots of supplemental Bible stuff at bedtime. I've found a variety of different, fun, and humorous tapes of Bible stories to play after tucking them in. I've added to this CDs with the Word being read aloud, as well as sung in worship. Those minutes before your children drift into sleep are a great time for capturing their attention with God's Word.

Drugged by Entertainment

Kids who excessively rent videos and gaming software to fill their free time are entertainment junkies. Most kids seem to have far too much time on their hands and money in their fists. For you who don't believe this, track the hours your children spend on computers, cable TV, video games, movie theatres, concerts, coffee shops, and mall time. As long as Junior lives under your roof, help him spend his money and his free time on more than his own pleasure.

Electronics

In 2001 U.S. consumers spent $633.6 million renting video games and a record-breaking $6 billion buying video game software, including PC software. PlayStation 2's "Grand Theft Auto 3" was the number one selling video game that year. Scary. And it's growing. Total retail sales by the U.S. toy industry in 2002 were a hefty $30.6 billion. Of this amount, $10.3 billion came from the sales of video games (Video Software Dealers' Association, 2002 Annual Report on the Home Entertainment Industry).

Don't be fooled into thinking all games are created equal. Tetris and PacMan are tiddlywinks compared to the R-rated content on the most popular electronic games. Parental guidance is suggested regarding the games your children are playing at home, at friends' homes, and at day care centers.

Friends and Punks

My children have a cluster (I said a cluster, not a herd) of amazing friends. These are comrades in the faith who lead them in the right direction. This doesn't just happen. It's up to us parents to direct our kids *toward* right friendships and *away* from dangerous ones. Don't leave it to chance. Churches are chock-full of kids you don't necessarily want hanging with your boys and girls. I wish I didn't have to say that, but I do. Every birthday party, overnight, and social invite is not an automatic "yes" for our children.

Be wise, and don't get pushed by some pushy parent into making your kid their little devil's companion. 1 Corinthians 15:33 so fittingly exhorts, *Do not be misled: "Bad company corrupts good character."* How reminiscent this is of the old saying, "If you lie with dogs, you get fleas!"

Don't play the fool. Don't ignore that still, small voice God's put right there in your spirit. It seems so unreasonable, but you just can't make peace with that party. You don't like a certain kid being around your kid. You hear fingernails scraping on a chalkboard every time that girl calls. The way that boy looks at you sets you on edge.

We've had barren, lonely days without an acceptable friend to be found for our boys. If this is where you find yourself at the moment, mine the gold right there and build the bond between siblings as you make the most of the solitude. Ride bikes, build Lego castles, read great books together, and serve those around you. Sow the right seeds in your children, and God will bring them good, godly friends.

Girls Don't Call Our Boys

Girls don't call our boys without receiving an invitation to do so. And on top of that, I screen all invites. Don't sing this tune: "I just don't know what to do. They're calling and calling, and I just give him the phone." Don't give him the phone. Try this: "Hello? (Sounds like a female voice.) Yes, you're calling for Junior. Oh, did Junior ask you to call? No? I'm sorry honey, but girls don't call our house. Bye." Works every time.

I refuse to open the door to the diabolical game of boyfriend/girlfriend nonsense. Our children need our protection from the onslaught of the media blitz which pushes them into the idea of romantic relationships at age ten. Flip through any popular magazine, and you're sure to find perfected photos of little girls looking sexy, often paired with boys so young that their peach fuzz hasn't yet surfaced. Childhood is a priceless, fleeting moment. Don't shorten it!

God's Word

God's Word is good enough for your kids! They need substantial Word times. The Bible, just as it is, is a great school book. We have many Bibles in our homes, but are we using them? Your kids may like to flip through magazines, fictional adventures, and fantasy novels, but do you ever just have them sit and read the Word? Have you trained them that the Word doesn't have to be condensed, sweetened, spun, and presented as happy cotton-candy story time? We are dumbing down our kids with Barnie's Bible and Silly Sue's Scriptures. It is the unadulterated, pure Word of God which, when planted and rooted in them, promises not to return void.

We read to our kids out of books like *Berenstain Bears* and *Thomas the Tank Engine*, but do we regularly open the Word to our children? This common, all-time best seller—the Bible—isn't just a book; it is a power tool for parents and children! Psalms 119:11 must be true of us and our kids: *I have hidden your Word in my heart that I might not sin against you.*

How can we hide God's Word in our heart if we've always got the TV on? (See Television, Television, and More Television, pp. 145–146.) If you can't control the TV, get rid of it. I believe it could prove to be one of the enemy's most effective tools to dwarf our homes and spiritual lives. A television is a neutral machine, not evil in itself. As much as I personally hate the thing, I can't get religious about a mechanical box. However, if it's out of control and is free to pump your house full of toxic waste, while robbing your family of God-life, relationships, and peace, then it becomes an enemy; and such enemies should be obliterated!

The Word of God crashes into 99.9 percent of what Hollywood is feeding us. *The food we need is food from the Word of God and the sustenance that we find on our knees in God's presence.* It's food that we cannot get out of a magazine. It's food that Oprah and Dr. Phil cannot give us.

Happy

"*Happy* Birthday! *Happy* Graduation! *Happy* Retirement! *Happy* Mothers' Day! *Happy* Anniversary!" "We wish you *happiness* always!" "I was so *happy* to hear . . .!" Hallmark loves the word "happy," and so do we. Folks spend lots of money wishing it upon others and even more time yearning for and pursuing it themselves. It's a lovely wish, but a rare reality, and for many in the world, it proves to be an elusive dream.

Happy means to be lucky, fortunate, and favored by circumstances. It implies contentment, gladness, and a feeling of great pleasure. It suggests that circumstances are exactly appropriate to the occasion. Mom and Dad, you and I know this Neverland doesn't exist for a large percentage of our lives. Why then do we insist on posturing our children toward this fantasy? It is one very tired (and broke!) parent who attempts to keep a child in a perpetual state of happiness. Rather, let's teach our children to choose contentment along life's paths, no matter the circumstances. Whether the sun is shining or the rain is falling, whether working or playing, whether hungry or full, a joyful disposition must be the standard for our boys and girls.

Household Chores Build Character

Children who are expected to complete house cleaning and maintenance tasks on a regular basis with a standard of excellence are pleasant to be around. Our kids have always been required to carry substantial weight around the house by doing chores. I believe it has built character in them. Along with a daily chore chart (see Chore Charts, pp. 129–130), they handle tasks like mowing, car washing, garage cleaning, food preparation, and any other stuff that has to be done on an as-needed basis. One of the first scriptures learned by our sons is one that many adults in our society still don't know: *If a man will not work, he shall not eat* (2 Thessalonians 3:10).

If little ones can walk, they can work. Toddlers can tidy up and organize stuff. Preschoolers qualify for helping in the kitchen, taking care of pets, and keeping their rooms neat. Those under ten (not just girls!) can vacuum, clean toilets, sweep, mop, and handle laundry or dishes. Gals, we've got a labor force in front of us if we'll do the training! Our children can release us into greater things as we train them in basic life skills. If your sons are chillin' while you hire others to push your mower and pull weeds, it's time for change at your house!

"I Gotta *GO!*"

One observation I've made in our church and many others we've visited refers to a practical illustration of mastering "self." There seems to be almost constant movement by youngsters in and out of corporate church meetings. My question is: How many times does a kid have to pee during a meeting? Perhaps being a leader in a local church, I'm in touch with how distracting it is for folks to be meandering in and out of the auditorium while someone is attempting to deliver a message, lead the music, or wait on the Holy Spirit to speak. My children know: You use the bathroom facilities before and after a meeting, not during. Unless they're sick and have a legitimate excuse, which is rare, they are to stay put. I guarantee if our kids were out playing ball, watching a DVD, or eating from a buffet at the local smorgasbord, they would not need to pee three times in an hour. Mom and Dad, let's not be such pushovers!

Incentives

Recently I took some time to develop an elaborate system of incentives to reward my nine- and twelve-year-old children for proper behavior in areas we'd been having some difficulty conquering. I looked at the plan and suddenly said, "No way. Shred it. My boys have a life of incentives every day. They are richly blessed already with friends, social gatherings at church, parties, movies, music, toys and trendy clothing, computer games, and books galore . . . to indulge them to a higher degree would be sin." When the children were preschoolers, I found success with incentive charts, and I felt they were appropriate. The trinkets they earned gave them small, reachable goals as they developed good habits and character traits. Now, however, I must expect more from these young-men-in-training!

Junk-food Kids

*400,000—number of deaths in 2000 caused by poor diet, making it the **Number 2 killer** after smoking.*

—Time, March 22, 2000

Throughout this book, I've touched on the topic of what we're feeding our families because what Junior's shoveling into his mouth is, quite frankly, a life or death matter. Check it out: Type 2 diabetes is deadly, leads to heart disease, and has reached epidemic proportions in our nation, but most often it can be avoided by improved lifestyle choices: a healthy diet and regular exercise. Look around. One-third of Americans are overweight or obese. At our house we've adopted a few principles to help keep us on track.

- As often as possible, eat food the way God made it, especially on the home front. Keep an arsenal on hand of everything that grows in the ground to counter the indiscriminate appetites of the immature.
- Require the daily eating of fresh, colorful, large salads with a variety of vegetables in the mix. Radishes, broccoli, sweet red peppers, sugar snap peas, purple cabbage, sprouts, sweet onion, spinach, romaine, cherry tomatoes, mushrooms, grated carrot, and turnip are some great salad veggies. I didn't say iceberg lettuce drowning in bottled ranch dressing with so many preservatives it will never die.
- Fresh or frozen fruit should be part of the *daily* diet. Smoothies made with frozen fruit are a super alternative to a bowl of ice cream.
- Ration minimal and rare portions of such processed foods as breakfast cereals, potato chips, white bread, and snack bars.
- Limit dairy products, juices, and sweets.
- Make water "the drink" at your house. Buy distilled if the taste of your tap water isn't nice.

We cannot feed our kids a standard American diet and expect them to excel. Perhaps you, Mom or Dad, didn't have the privilege of learning this as a lifestyle while growing up. It's not too late!

Pioneer a better path of "eating to live" for your family! Before you know it, these forays into nutritious eating will become lifelong habits. Dig into one of the resources

I've listed at the back of the book (*Eat to Live*) under "For Further Reading," and your interest may be piqued.

Kids in the Main Meeting at Church

I really do believe kids can absorb a whole lot more than most folks give them credit for. I've often kept my boys with me in the main meetings at church because I think it's a valuable time for them to hear from godly men and women and to catch what the Holy Spirit is doing in our midst. I've also chosen to keep our kids with us during the corporate expression of worship while the music team is leading us in beautiful songs of praise. Even at 18 months, children can be taught to sit through this time and mind their manners.

However, I never want to bring legalism into our lives as people of God. The church our family calls home gives us liberty to function with our children as we decide what's best for them. From birth to about age twelve, there is a nursery or class available for them to be part of if the kids are well behaved and the parents volunteer to serve regularly in some capacity. We can choose to place them in the age-appropriate class or keep them with us in the meeting, assuming we keep them quiet so they are not distracting others with cute antics or fussing.

Some parents feel strongly that they want their kids with them at all times in every meeting. Other parents are more flexible about this issue and keep their children with them during special meetings, etc. Newcomers almost always utilize our kids' classes. We don't sit in awe of folks whose kids sit silent with them, or look down on those whose kids attend every children's ministry class. We are free to grow in Christ and to lead our children as God leads us.

Kittens, Puppies, and Other Pets

A common misconception, especially among westernized parents, is that "kids need a dog or a cat or a pot-bellied pig or a pony." Why do children need one more thing we know we'll offer to do for them? If Junior can't pick up his clothes, keep his toys tidy, bathe without a fight, or remember to take out the trash, what makes us think he will care adequately for a living, breathing animal?

Before you invest in a pet, make sure your child has earned the privilege and has time in his schedule to walk, play with, feed, clean up after, let out, let in, brush, and paper train little Spot with a happy heart. Don't forget about shedding, fences, dog beds, shots, allergies, travel cages, balls, bones, special dietary needs, collars, licenses, yard issues, middle-of-the-night barking, and the expense of it all.

Let's (NOT) Go to the Mall

Have you noticed that America's greatest indoor spectator sport, next to movies and eating out, is shopping? Let's discourage our kids from following the herd to the mall on weekends for entertainment and distraction. A mall is a place to dodge land mines. From lewd displays in lingerie shop windows and hoodlums hunkered in groups to half-dressed teens making whoopee in the hallways, it's a shocking scene.

Added to this is the absolute torture of eyeballing utterly gorgeous displays of everything a heart could possibly desire, but can't afford. Why bother? You can buy ice cream at the grocery store without such agony! The path to the mall is littered with deeply indebted and insecure people longing to validate themselves by wearing the right brands and exterior style to mimic a fickle culture where fashions change daily. Sounds like a great place for ordinary kids, but not yours or mine. Let's refuse to make our kids into mall rats.

Managers or Molders?

Most modern men and women had worldly models or no models at all from which to learn effective, godly parenting skills. Perhaps that's why so many drift into the mode of *managing* their children's lives instead of carefully *molding* them. The mass populous of our nation's parents can buy school supplies, complete enrollment paperwork, pack lunches, cart kids here and there, set up play dates, bathe, and put their kids to bed every day for eighteen years or so. This illustrates managing a young life, but molding is a different ball game altogether and it demands a parent's wholehearted devotion.

Shifting gears from managing to molding is no small endeavor. It's a bit like taking ownership of a business, rather than simply being an employee. An owner has bought in with all of his emotional and financial resources and is completely responsible for the outcome of the business; in contrast, an employee's ties are very loose and perhaps even temporary. An employee operates at surface level with very little invested and with options always open. An owner is fully committed to the end. Nannies may manage, grandparents may nurture, aunts and uncles may bless, but parents must mold, fashion, and form.

Marketing

When I buy myself a coffee at Starbucks, why must I feel compelled to purchase trinkets or "their own little drinks" for my youngsters? This cunning scheme of marketers is extremely effective, and you can't blame them for promoting such a profit-bolstering plan. They know us better than we know ourselves, and they obviously know how standard it is for us worldly parents to indulge our children.

We are subtly made to feel as though we owe an endless series of privileges to our children. Gradually, it can become expected and, worse yet, demanded by our little tykes. On special occasions, I enjoy surprising my sons with their own special treat when we're out together, but it can never be demanded by them. Let's clear our vision and identify this imposition as the absolute nonsense that it is.

Money Matters

When our boys hit age twelve, we start them on an allotment program based on the sum of what we spend in a year on clothing, hair cuts, entertainment, and a few wants divided by twelve. We add 20 percent, which is tithe and savings, and give this final amount to them on the first day of each month. They're required to tithe 10 percent and save 10 percent, although they usually choose to do more than that in each category.

For a given year, they learn to keep an account, recording on the computer any deposits made or expenses paid with receipts. They're responsible to pay for all their clothing, hair cuts, entertainment, and wants. This budget doesn't even come close to providing all the extras, so they're forced to get odd jobs and be creative to earn extra cash for things like Kids Camp and fancy brands of clothing. It's fun to see them take ownership, shop the sales, and learn to love the discount stores.

I no longer stress over who got new shoes or didn't, who needs this or that, etc. The boys rise to the occasion and seem to really enjoy it. They learn to live within their means because Mom's bank doesn't extend credit. If they blow their money on an expensive pair of shoes, it's their fault if they haven't got any socks to wear! I enjoy filling in the gaps at holidays when Daddy and I buy them some special items, but other than that, the buck stops with them.

Movies

In the U.S. in 2001, $7 billion was spent on VHS tape rentals with *Meet the Parents* holding at number one, and $1.4 billion was spent on DVD rentals with *Unbreakable* in the top position (Video Software Dealers' Association, 2002 Annual Report on the Home Entertainment Industry). That's a whole lot of extra time spent in front of the tube, consuming a whole bunch of nonsense. America's late fees on videos and DVDs combined would likely feed entire poor populations in some third-world countries!

Let's take inventory in our homes and honestly evaluate how we're spending our free time and extra cash. Many parents don't realize that they're actually paying to poison their own children with profanity, sexually suggestive content, wrong mind-sets, and unhelpful worldly thinking. Don't be shy about preserving the innocence of your children through close monitoring of their viewing habits. Perhaps it's time for a ruthless detox in the area of entertainment at your house!

No-Pout/No-Whine Zone

At the Mira home, children wake up cheerful or they go back to bed. This policy works wonders for us. We, as parents of leaders, must reject the "Eeyore pouting syndrome" of moaning and speaking negatively about any aspect of our glorious, blessed life in a first-world nation.

This goes hand-in-hand with the issue of whining. Whining is when kids put pressure on Mom and Dad to get something they want. In our home, if a child asks once for something and Dad or Mom says "no," that's it. Let's make sure we're not training our kids to ask us twenty times for something until we explode. That's not love. Make your house a no-pout and no-whine zone.

No Television in Bedrooms

I ban television in bedrooms unless Junior has strep throat and wants to watch a video while quarantined! Televisions are not optional furniture fixtures in our kids' bedrooms—ever. (See Computers with Internet Access in Bedrooms, pp. 131–132 and Television, Television, and More Television, pp. 145–146 for my philosophy on these matters).

One, Two, Three . . . Time-outs Mean I'm Free!

Three more seconds for your child to live in rebellion is nonsense! Counting to three as we wait for a right response from our kids and sentencing them to time-outs for their wrongdoing doesn't teach our children quick obedience or respect for authority. You're the authority *now*, not three seconds from now. I didn't say the shout-at-the-top-of-your-lungs-and-throw-things boss. Our children need calm, loving, courageous leadership.

I think time-outs are foolish because delayed obedience is disobedience. Why give Susie ten more minutes to sit and think about her rebellion? Instead of sitting her in a chair, why not put her to work?! If you fell for the "counting to three" thing or nonsensical time-outs, shake it off, repent, and take back the ground you turned over to the adversary. Don't teach your boy or girl to thumb their nose at you for even a millisecond!

As parents, I believe we're setting the pattern for how our children will relate to the living God. What a privilege to prepare them to readily embrace truth and *quickly* obey their Lord with a happy heart! What a tragedy if we're found to be the cause of their delayed obedience and casual attitude toward sin by allowing them to ignore our repeated pleas for compliance! By our permissive parenting in ignoring their offenses, failing to follow through on our threats, or trivializing sinful patterns, we teach our kids not to respond to the still, small voice of the Lord.

Outdoor Play

A recent article in *Readers Digest* estimated children's outdoor play at an average of about an hour every seven days. Whatever happened to kids playing outside for hours of creative fun, with their only interruption being Mom yelling, "Dinner's ready!"? I have a few ideas about the matter. It could be that formal education has hi-jacked our lives. Seven-year-old boys walk down our street under the weight of heavy backpacks after an eight-hour day of classes. They can't play in the sunshine because they've got homework until seven or eight. But, that's only part of the problem.

It could be that with nobody home when Junior and Susie get off the bus, they're instructed to stay inside so they're "safe" until Mom or Dad get home from work. Or perhaps the unchecked electronic activities are just so tempting that they consume any free hours left in the day. Whatever the case may be, I'm voting for outdoor play to no longer be an option, but rather a command from Mom and Dad.

I approach it something like this at our house: "Boys, it's time to play outside. If I hear any whining or see you sitting out on the driveway doing nothing, then I'll provide you with some hard labor from the extra chore chart. Have fun out there, whether you like it or not. Get creative, and I want to see movement! You better be sweating from all the fun you're having or else!" It works!

Overnights

It's Friday night, and the natives are restless. You feel it in the air. TGIF EVERYONE! School books are stashed and hopes are runnin' high! You know what's coming. "Can I stay overnight at Jack's house? There's a slumber party at Jessica's." It's a regular part of life with school-age kids from Australia to South Africa and everywhere in between! It sounds innocent enough . . . snacks, sleeping bags, pillows, friends, and frolic. Aw shucks, if I could just stay surface level on this thing called overnights!

But my overly active mind begins to question: What are the values held in Jack's house? Are there older, possibly perverse siblings with unsavory friends there, too? Who'll be sleeping next to my boy? What reading material is lying around Jessica's house? Any movies gonna be shown? Hmm. Who else is invited, and will they bring contraband? How much sugar will be consumed? How much sleeping will actually happen? Sleepovers are fine with me, if I'm invited too! Ninety-nine percent of our kids' overnights happen at our house. That's peace for me.

Potlucks and Parties

Our children need certain social graces which are rooted in a respect for others. We shouldn't allow raucous little children the right to race their way to the head of food lines, in front of adults and other mature guests who are present at potlucks or parties. How rude of them to grub everything their hearts desire, even touching things they decide not to take with no thought for those behind them in the queue! What are we thinking by teaching them they can rifle through all the desserts with their mucky little fingers, slobbering, hoarding, picking through the healthy stuff to pile on the starches and carbs while their impotent parents sit idly by, watching but unmoved?

Wise adults won't leave the children to rule. Caring adults get involved. Kindly impose regulations when necessary. There are occasions when a citizen's arrest is absolutely appropriate, and if it happens to your kid, don't get your nose out of joint.

Protective Boundaries

Three of my sons had some special time at a friend's house which included a video I wasn't privy to and hadn't approved. When someone spilled the beans, I knew I had to take action, so I did. As they remembered this "unjust" incident from days gone by, my three older boys would exclaim in stereo, "You spanked us all for watching one PG movie at the Mitchell's house. That was ridiculous!"

The firm, protective policy in place was always to ask permission if a video was going to be viewed. They didn't ask. They chose to disobey my command. They rationalized away my boundary with immaterial "case evidence" about its rating, popularity, etc. It wasn't about the movie's righteousness. It was the principle of the matter. It was about guarding their innocence into the future and their casual attitude toward my crystal-clear guidelines.

Puppy Love

There's entirely too much romancing going on in the church! Be ruthless with this one. You've got leverage, and the power is in your hands. Temporary "seasonal romance" between Christian kids is not only unhealthy, but dangerous. If marriage isn't planned, what right do our kids have to be holding hands with and kissing someone else's future spouse? This style of relating copies the world's pattern and sets our kids up for moral failure, as well as teaching them a pattern of temporary loves which, I believe, weakens future marriage foundations. I hope I'm not ranting, but I feel strongly about this, especially in light of so many teen pregnancies and sexually transmitted diseases, even among Christians.

We've got to teach our sons and daughters to let God bring their spouse, rather than enabling them to practice a lifestyle of prowling and pursuing a mate. I tell the young ladies in my life, "If you want a cute guy, buy a poster." (An appropriate poster, of course!) "Cute" doesn't equip or prepare you for life's storms. It doesn't pledge allegiance to forever. "Cute" is an incidental, frivolous, and ludicrous reason for giving anyone attention—unless they're toddlers or puppies.

Quest for Cell-phone Freedom

Pre-teens and cell phones? You don't have to be a genius to know this could be a recipe for disaster, depending on the character of the teen in question. At night before I go to bed, I have a habit of checking to make sure all the doors and windows are closed and locked securely. Personally, I'm not comfortable with a door I can't lock when I close my eyes at night. A cell phone in the hands of an impressionable and not-necessarily-so-trustworthy young person could prove to be an unsecured entryway for unsavory influences and unacceptable friendships.

This is most definitely one serious tool of privilege, which must be earned by a long obedience in the same direction. I've said before, "If they can't afford it, they shouldn't have it." I would take it one step further and say, "If they *can* afford it, but *can't* handle it, they don't need it." As I see it, 99.9 percent of children under driving age shouldn't have a cell phone, and no child with an attitude should have one, even if he's independently wealthy!

This topic brings to mind a pretty wild story: When our family's monthly cell phone bills arrive, inevitably, there are erroneous charges on any one of our five accounts. Get ready, Mr. Cingular, 'cause here I come! Though our children pay their own bills, I go to bat for them as needed. They call me "The Negotiator." I can always count on spending a good thirty minutes appealing, haggling, and keeping these guys honest.

One particular gentleman commented on how small these discrepancies were (about $7.00 that month—hey, that's two lattes!) compared to the phone call he had just taken from a frantic mother. It seems that her son had downloaded an entire movie by MMode, and she received the bill for $3200.00! That kid has too much time on his hands and probably several character issues that need work. My question was: "What's he doing with a cell phone anyhow?"

Reading Good Books Is a Priority

Frivolous fiction and fantasy book series are breeding like rabbits these days. They can be unhelpful to our leaders-in-training. I don't want to be religious and put my kids in a straight jacket, but I ration the fiction to a large degree. Don't "just be glad they're reading" like the rest of society's experts. I think it would be wise of us to scan what our kid has his nose in on a rainy day and beef up that reading material if he leans toward flimsy little books and magazines that are meaningless and don't challenge him or build his vocabulary. Our kids are expected to be reading non-fiction continually, interspersed with fiction that they like which also matches our values. I think you'll find your kids' vocabularies are stretched and their knowledge broadened by such a plan.

Siblings Are Valued

A kingdom household is a safe place where our greatest fans live. All-for-one and one-for-all. Kindness to siblings is expected in our home. The oldest doesn't bully, and the youngest isn't favored. We are a team. We support each other verbally, emotionally, and spiritually. Don't allow cruelty amongst your children, and make sure the "baby" of the family isn't pampered. I think pandering to the "caboose" in the family is far too common a blind spot for lots of parents. This practice fosters resentment in the camp and creates walls of division between the kids.

Teen Labor Transitions

Once our kids hit adolescence, they should have people lining up to hire them! As our boys began to take jobs outside the home in their teens, they began to carry less and less weight around our home. They graduated from bathroom cleaning and other household dailies to bearing the weight of their college studies, employers' needs, and increased ministry responsibilities. Yet, they've always been on call for big jobs like landscaping, house painting, building decks, and other projects for which Dad needs them.

It's been a natural progression of their growth into manhood with their own spheres to manage. Our first and second-born kids found themselves managing their own homes at ages eighteen and nineteen, respectively. They rented rooms to friends and made chore plans for their buddies! The ol' days of checking off chore charts had helped to prepare them for the tomorrows of running their own businesses and providing for their households.

Television, Television, and More Television

Why do I hate the television *sit,* I mean "set"? For one, I'm convinced this addictive contraption keeps children indoors, to their detriment. The relentless advertising encourages mall time, fashion fixation, and money spent unwisely, which leads to indebtedness. It spouts out perversity 24/7, poisoning our impressionable children with worldly mind-sets about morality, diet, romance, sexuality, parental authority, and relationships in marriage, to mention a few, thus belittling the biblical values we're fighting so vehemently to uphold.

Even more importantly perhaps, I'm persuaded that this witty invention has fostered the breakdown of family relationships due to massive amounts of solitary time spent "together" in front of the tube night after night after night.

Training Takes Time

Some friends of ours had an unruly pooch. They did some research and found a training school for dogs in their area. For a healthy sum, their puppy was enrolled in an around-the-clock regimen of tedious training. At the end of two weeks, the owners met with the trainers to get instructions for following the same regimen at home in order to see ultimate success with the program. They learned that training the pooch takes time. It seems this nation needs a similar program for kids! Many peoples' dogs are more obedient and mannerly than their own flesh and blood children.

Building practical skills into our child's portfolio is also time-consuming. We must first teach, then re-teach, then follow up and inspect the job they've done when we're training our children. Standing over them nag, nag, nagging and grumbling is not training. I've tried it. It's not very effective.

A child will not clean a floor perfectly the first, second, or third time around, especially when he's seven years old. We must patiently walk him through the process and pull him through to victory and maturity. We have to put ourselves in their places and realize that we've all had to be trained in many things. It's never automatic, and we must be patient, not harsh. If we cross the line and become frazzled and rough with our kids, we exasperate them. Don't forget that children are tender, and we can crush them. If we've indulged in such sinful behavior, we should lead by sincerely repenting to our kids and asking for their forgiveness. Then warmly, with humility, try again.

Unholy Alliances with Our Children

Enabling mothers are doing harm to their children and to society. Have you noticed how many convicts live with their mothers? If you have the stomach for the nightly news, you'll observe murderers, pedophiles, and drug addicts hiding out with their mothers when the police come to arrest them. These are mothers who have provided their sons and daughters with a resting place for their rebellion and a safe place to indulge in sin.

In the name of undying love, these mothers have made a den for thieves. This brand of "love" will eventually take a child to his ruin.

Think for a moment. Do you offer the same detrimental enabling on a smaller scale to your child? Do you reserve a hiding place, a comfortable place for his sin? If so, be ruthless with this insidious tendency in your life. Proverbs 19:18 warns, *Discipline your son, for in that there is hope; do not be a willing party to his death.* Be careful to offer your child true love that builds his life in God, not counterfeit love which in the end will bring destruction. Don't be "nicer" than God.

Unusual Manners

Children with bad manners won't get very far. There is something to be said for appropriate behavior and social graces, even for boys. Along with proper greeting of adults mentioned above (Greetings) and proper responses to adults touched on below ("Yes, Sir!"), I believe there's value in kids chewing with their mouths closed and refraining from burping and speaking of unpleasant things at the table. Let's teach our kids not to "shovel" with their eating utensils, to always thank the cook for preparing the delicious food, and never for even a second to complain about what's being served whether at home or as a guest at someone's house. Let's also teach our kids to answer the phone properly, take their hands out of their pants, thank friends' parents who've hosted them, and offer to clean up anytime, anywhere when they see a mess and can be of assistance. Add to this list of suggestions anything you feel strongly about in the area of social skills, even if no one else is requiring it of their kids.

Voice Your Disapproval with Schools

Martin Luther said, "I am afraid that the schools will prove the very gates of hell, unless they diligently labor in explaining the Holy Scriptures and engraving them on the hearts of the youth." As parents we need to let our voices be heard at our public schools. The state does not own your children, but they want to, and they will if you don't rise up. We need to take our place and kindly, but firmly, say, "No more. No, my boy's not going to watch that movie. No, my boy's not going to read that book. No, my daughter is not going to that dance. And no, co-ed camping trips are not for us." Let your voice be heard and challenge the moral vacuum of our public school system.

Written Communication

Teach your children to weave a tapestry of beautiful words that bless and build up others. Thank-you notes should not be optional. Mom was right! Thank-yous can help our children build the muscles of gratefulness and thoughtfulness. By writing notes my boys work out their vocabulary, spelling, sentence structure, punctuation, artistry, and penmanship or typing skills, all-in-one!

For little ones just starting out, I recommend the fill-in-the-blank type of thank-yous. It's easy to create these with fun paper on any home computer, or you can purchase them ready-made. Special note cards or personalized stationery can be a great motivator for your older children.

Gifts aren't the only reason for writing. Teach your kids to appreciate grandparents, workers in your local church, war veterans, community service people in your life, and others who would love to find real mail in their box!

As in other life disciplines, don't settle for ordinary when your child is capable of *so much more!* Hand-written, personal notes are rare in our day, but always well-received! Sloppily written text filled with redundant wording, equals laziness. Add horizontal lines with a ruler to help your kids succeed in the neatness category. Rough drafts are often a good exercise and give Mom or Dad an opportunity to review and offer creative input. Have a thesaurus and dictionary handy as tools for successful expression.

I enjoy making copies of my sons' best completed notes to file in a memory box. If you happen to home school, these qualify as a record of meaningful schoolwork. Either way, you will have imparted a very valuable life skill.

X-rated Clothing

Friends, if your little girl can't afford the second half of that shirt, don't buy the first half! If your boys' pants are hanging off their rears, make them wear a belt or they lose the pants. I don't care if we live in a beach culture where the weather is 110 degrees. We live in a holy kingdom culture where "radical" means dressing modestly, so we don't cause others to stumble. Make war on inappropriate clothing. Tell your sons, "Boys, be careful. Watch for all the spandex; there may be a predator in there." Tell your girls, "Stop it! Peel that lycra off your loins, and buy some clothes that fit!"

"Yes, Sir!"

In the South, it's common to hear children answer elders with "yes, sir" or "no, ma'am" when they're spoken to. Fifteen years ago, we came across such a family with this unusual (to us!) habit, and we liked it. We adopted the practice with our sons and have made it a requirement inside and outside of our home. "Yeah," "dude," "sweet," and "whatever" aren't good enough responses for a leader to be giving. A respectful and honorable reply will turn heads and give glory to God. Some close friends have taught their kids to answer with a "Yes, Dad" or "Yes, Mom" to affirm they've heard their parent's command. Elders and other adults in our lives should be shown unusual respect by our sons. You don't have to do it like someone else, but find a way to implement this principle of respectful response in your children.

Zip the Lip

The Word of God tells us plainly that, *If anyone is never at fault in what he says, he is a perfect man, able to keep his whole body in check* (James 3:2). We've got to help our children to master this restless muscle of the tongue. Why should we settle for street talk when God has given us a vast vocabulary from which to choose? Don't laugh, but I think "hate" is a very strong statement. It's used in our home only when we're talking about sin and the devil. We do not hate onions, hard work, or siblings. If we do, we will not have a happy day! "Sucks" is not fitting for an up-and-coming leader, and "shut up" is a slap in the face and builds walls between people. Tolerating this terminology will not bring out the best in our children. It doesn't matter what "everyone else" is saying. Hold a high standard with your verbiage and the verbiage of your kids.

Change Us, Lord

Could this be a prayer from our hearts?

"Help us to be idealistic, Lord; we cry out to You. We are sitting here feeling convicted, stirred, and provoked. We ask You to breathe on us. Cut off with Your axe what has to go. We ask You to sharpen us and change us! We cry out to our source and our fountain, to the One who loves us and is for us and not against us. We cry out to the One who has amazing plans for our welfare, to give [us] a future and a hope, according to Jeremiah 29:11 (NKJV).

"God, we repent right now of our wrong mind-sets and of those things we are imbibing that bear bad fruit in our lives. We repent of any sinful ways we've embraced and of accepting roles the world has offered us. We will run after You, God! We ask You to change us today. A man or a woman can't change us. A message can't change us, but You can change us by Your Spirit. We don't want to leave any stone unturned in this process. We want to be ruthless with ourselves. We don't want to live dull lives of compromise. We want to live lives of purpose, like Moses. We want to be, and to raise, no ordinary generation. May it be so through Jesus Christ."

FOR FURTHER READING

This is a list of some key books that have enriched, impacted, equipped, or simply encouraged me along my journey of nurturing and training young leaders at home.

Dobson, James. *Dare to Discipline*. Wheaton, IL: Tyndale House Publishers, 1973.

Fugate, Richard J. *What the Bible Says about Child Training*. Foundation for Biblical Research, 1999.

Fuhrman, J. M.D. *Eat To Live*. New York: Little, Brown and Company, Time Warner Book Group, 2003.

Gatto, John T. *Dumbing Us Down*. Philadelphia: New Society Publishers, 1992.

Harris, Gregg. *The Christian Home School*. Noble Publishing Associates, 1988.

Harvey, E.F & L. *Soul Sculpture*. North Carolina: Harvey Christian Publishing, 1967.

Moore, R. & D. *Home Grown Kids*. W Publishing Group, 1984.

Pearl, Michael and Debi. *To Train Up a Child*. Tennessee: Self Published, 1994.

Pride, Mary. *The Way Home*. Illinois: Crossway Books. 1985.

Shackelford, L. & White, S. *A Survivor's Guide to Home Schooling*. Illinois: Crossway Books, 1988.

Young, Helen M. *Children Won't Wait*. Texas: Brownlow Publishing Company, Inc. 1985.

To Order Additional Copies of

No Ordinary Child

Unlocking the Leader Within Your Child

Have your credit card ready and visit:

www.denisemira.com or e-mail us at contact@denisemira.com